App Secrets: How to Create a Milli(

Written by: Sean Casto

MW00993639

Disclaimer

The purpose of this book is to educate and entertain. The author or publisher does not guarantee that anyone following the techniques, suggestions, tips, ideas, or strategies will become successful. The author and publisher shall have neither liability or responsibility to anyone with respect to any loss or damage caused or alleged to be caused, directly or indirectly by the information contained in this book.

TABLE OF CONTENTS

ACKNOWLEDGMENT

I dedicate this book to my father. The best gift I ever received was being given the father I had when I was born. I would not be where I am today without your love and mentoring.

I cannot thank the following people enough for the impact they have had on my life both personally and professionally. These marketing legends shaped and expanded my mindset towards business and marketing: Tony Robbins, Russell Brunson, Joe Polish, Dan Sullivan, Dan Kennedy, Peter Diamandis, Sean Stephenson, Brandon Burchard, Lewis Howes, Jay Abraham, James Wedmore, Neil Patel, Vignesh Kumar, Seth Godin, and Noah Kagan.

Special thanks to App marketing legends: Chad Mureta, George Berkowski, Steve Young, Gabriel Machuret, and Carter Thomas for paving the way for others to turn their App dreams and reality.

I am truly standing on the shoulders of giants.

INTRODUCTION

Today, it's easier to build an App than ever before. New technologies are introduced regularly making it easier, faster and cheaper to develop profitable Apps. If you want to build an App yet feel overwhelmed with where to start, or if ready to take your existing app to the next level, you're in the right place. Anyone who ever built an empire, created something incredible, launched a billion-dollar App, disrupted industries or changed the world, stood where you stand today. At the beginning.

Throughout this book, we will journey through the most successful Apps and what they all have in common and discover the formula for true success. We'll go step-by-step through the system and framework that took me eight years to perfect. What I discovered is success leaves clues. You do not need to reinvent the wheel. There are things that work and things that don't. I'll show you a path that ensures your App is successful and help you avoid the pitfalls others faced, wasting both time and money.

When the App Store first opened, it took four years for Instagram to become the first ever billion-dollar App. One year later, Uber and Airbnb joined the billion-dollar App club. Today, a new App reaches the million-dollar mark every month, while billion-dollar valuations occur practically every six months. This book reveals the ESSENTIAL strategies, blueprints, frameworks and habits differentiating these million-dollar Apps from the 90% that fail every year!

Too many aspiring App creators are trapped in traditional ways of thinking. Most of these "entrepreneurs" go an entire year without changing a thing. They work very hard and wonder why their App failed to generate the downloads they anticipated.

Every day, we hear about people who control their own destiny, own their dreams, reap huge benefits and, in many cases, change the world for the better. Many think these people are just lucky. They believe it's unattainable, that those who succeed have some special powers enabling them to achieve success. They don't.

Something I learned in my eight years of research is that NONE of the most successful App creators are SMARTER than you or me. They don't possess any special powers that got them to where they are today. The creators of every billion-dollar App get out of bed in the morning, just like we do.

Like Hollywood celebrities and Olympic athletes, they are all ordinary people doing extraordinary things. These Titans have figured out something too many of us have overlooked: The world's biggest problems are the world's biggest business opportunities. If you want to be a billionaire, then help a billion people.

Just a few hundred years ago, the only people that could really spark change and create something, were the kings and queens of the world. Fast-forward and we live in a time where any one of us can take a problem that we are truly passionate about, and truly care about, and solve it. Today each of us has the capability to affect millions of lives!

We have a world of information at our fingertips. Your smartphone has more power than the supercomputer that NASA used to launch a man to the moon and bring him back safely. There is more information and power in your pocket than the United States government had just 60 years ago. You literally have the tools to solve the world's biggest problems. Couple those with billion-dollar ambitions and your world is limitless.

If you incorporate my key ESSENTIALS in this book, I have no doubt that you will reach extraordinary success. Once you understand the framework all top Apps incorporate, you will be unstoppable. While reading this book, I encourage you to see the potential the App industry has for

INTRODUCTION

YOU. This book is intended for everyone however if you are a seasoned app professional and want to get straight to the beef you may jump to Chapter 6.

I want you to know, the purpose of this book is to increase the quality of your life and to give you an opportunity to explore new ways of looking at what is possible for you as part of the lucrative and exciting App industry.

If you're reading this and feel discouraged, I'm here to show you that our industry works. I will prove, beyond a doubt, that creating a million-dollar (or even a billion-dollar App) is not only possible, but repeatable. This book will be your roadmap to success.

As the late Steve Jobs said, "Here's to the crazy ones, the misfits, the rebels, the troublemakers, the round pegs in the square holes. The ones who see things differently. They're not fond of rules. You can quote them, disagree with them, glorify or vilify them. But the only thing you can't do is ignore them, because they change things. They push humanity forward, and while some may see them as the crazy ones. We see genius."

"Because the ones who are crazy enough to think that they can change the world, are the ones who do."

My Mission Is To Empower
One Million App Creators

Just like you, at my core I am an App developer and marketer. When I first started out in the Mobile App Industry back in 2009, I built and launched a half-dozen Apps on my own. I also worked for an App development studio. Today, I am the CEO and Founder of the Premier App Marketing Agency, PreApps. I have been honored to work with thousands of App creators, reach millions of downloads, in 80 countries and across 24 different categories.

We helped launch and market Apps, from nothing to millions of downloads and sales. I've worked with incredibly successful million-dollar Apps including: Mr. Jump, OverKill 2, MeisterTask and billion-dollar Apps including: Cheetah Mobile's Security Master which has more than 550,000,000 downloads to date.

But I didn't start off working with billion-dollar Apps. When I first started out I failed in just about every imaginable way. My failures helped me understand the struggles many of you face building, launching, and marketing an App. When Thomas Edison was asked by his biographer, "What was it like to fail more than 100x trying to invent a battery to store electricity?" His reply was epic. "What do you mean failure? I now know 100 ways NOT to store electricity!" Like Edison, I now know more than 100 ways NOT to build and market an App. I've faced many barriers on my journey and I've most likely faced the same challenges you meet daily.

One of my first unique barriers came as a ten year-old boy. I was told that I had a learning disability called dyslexia. This disability caused me to sometimes see words and numbers backwards. Growing up, I had trouble reading. Math presented unique challenges. I became afraid to speak in public and failed more exams than I care to remember.

I thought that having dyslexia meant that I was stupid. I felt inferior failing so many tests and assumed having dyslexia meant I was destined to be a failure. My greatest fear was being realized — the same fear we all share — a fear of NEVER being successful.

Growing up, I had a burning desire to prove everyone wrong. I wanted to create success by building something of value for the world. I knew the typical nine-to-five grind was not for me.

I wanted to live a lifestyle most only read about, watch in movies, or see on Facebook. I wanted to turn my App dreams into reality. To have others love what I created, be financially free, travel the world and pursue my passions. I wanted to have children someday and support them, like my father supported me. I needed to be the kind of father they could be proud of.

In College, dyslexia made it very difficult to learn computer programming. While studying full time and trying to get my business started, things took a turn for the worse. My co-founder lost faith in what we were doing and my startup at the time failed. I persisted, but after my fifth failed startup, I didn't feel I was getting anywhere. I wasn't fulfilling my dream. Perhaps you have felt the same way or have run into a similar disillusionment.

I was sitting in the living room of my apartment in Boston, feeling utterly defeated, sick to my stomach and out of money. I had no idea how to pay my bills that month. There was a shooting pain in my stomach and a heavy weight relentlessly pushed down on my back. My whole body shook, I was in so much pain. That pain was sheer frustration. I was that ten-year year-old boy again, destined for failure.

Then, something incredible happened!

My mentor shared a message with me that profoundly shaped my future forever. It was a video from 1990 of an interview with a young Steve Jobs when he was building Apple. Jobs said, "Everything around you, that you call life, was created by people, that were no smarter than you…. You can change it, you can influence it, and you can build your own things that other people can use. Once you learn that, you'll never be the same again."

It was then I felt a surge of passion run through my being, right to my very core. I had this epiphany! At that very moment I realized successful million and billion-dollar App creators didn't have any special powers. They were no smarter than me! They put their pants on one leg at a time, just like everyone else. They were simply more resourceful and understood the App industry differently from everyone else. I knew if they could do it, so could I. And that's when I made a change.

To be successful, I must model the actions of App creators who succeeded before me. I'd been trying to figure it all out on my own. I was trying to reinvent the wheel like 95% of people in the App business try to do and end up failing. I now knew I needed to model others' success. NOW there was no turning back!

I set out on a journey to uncover the proven processes, systems, and frameworks of how to create a million-dollar App. Over an eight year period, I studied and interviewed dozens of the top million and billion-dollar App makers on the market. I read all the top App marketing books and took the best courses in the industry. I broke things down and studied the essential traits that led these people to succeed. These traits which generated millions of downloads and drove significant sales for others in the market.

What I've realized is that there are many similarities in the strategies of the apps that reached profound growth, and enormous success. I started to combine the proven systems and processes that I learned to create proven techniques such as the "Skyrocket Method," the "Viral App

Blueprint," and the "10x Revenue Model" to help ANY app achieve explosive growth and success.

When I started using these strategies, my results went THROUGH THE ROOF!

I had to know these systems would work for every App. So I continued to incorporate them repeatedly with other Apps. I had to be sure it wasn't a fluke. As a result these Apps received global exposure and reached millions of downloads. These Apps became worldwide App celebrities, market leaders in their categories and many were featured by Apple.

I've now worked with more 3,250 Apps to help them achieve over 550,000,000 downloads. Empowering others to build and launch successful Apps, completely transformed my life.

If there is anything I want you to get out of this, it's this. ANYONE can hit it big in this industry, and app success is in fact repeatable. There is a formula to do this and a proven path to success that the most successful apps on the market incorporate, that very FEW know about. Strategies you can use to get the same results. But you have to follow the patterns and traits of the most successful apps to get there.

By following the methods I teach you here, I built an amazing life for myself. I pursue my passions, travel the world and help others succeed. As a consultant, I have dedicated my life to empowering fellow developers like YOU with the tools, knowledge, and resources to position your App for success. I genuinely want YOU to succeed in this business, and help you change the course of your success for the better. It's now my mission to empower 1,000,000 new successful app creators.

It's my hope YOU are one of them.

PART ONE

THE APP

SUCCESS MINDSET

CHAPTER 1

THE MILLION DOLLAR APP CLUB

We have become more reliant on our smartphone than any other device in human history. This has sparked the greatest opportunity for accessible instant products and services the world has ever seen. According to a report by Kleiner Perkins, the average smartphone user looks at their phone an estimated 150 times per day. For more avid users it's estimated at 215 times per day.

For many, their smartphone has become an extension of their body. Used every few minutes to check the time, listen to music, get directions, text friends, browse the Internet, and check emails. To give you some perspective, outside of a person's wallet or watch, there has never been a single device that a person has carried with them 24/7 since the dawn of time. The smartphone is part of the human environment. While some view this as invasive, it has brought us an incredible opportunity. A 2013 Harris Interactive study found 75% of people keep their smartphone within five feet of them at ALL times. We can now create a product or service that impacts peoples' lives 24/7 and know that it will be no more than five feet away from a user at any time. Apps have become the most powerful, connecting, opinion moving, stress relieving and purchasing forces on the planet today.

Why Apps?

According to the analytics firm App Annie, the global App economy will be worth $6.3 trillion dollars by 2021. During that same time frame, the App user base will grow from 3.4 to 6.3-billion. The time users spend in those Apps, will more than double to 3.5-trillion hours in 2021, from 1.6-trillion in 2016.

The App Industry is the new modern-day gold rush that everyone wants in on. There are 3,000 new Apps introduced into the marketplace every day with new Apps hitting the million-dollar valuation mark monthly.

What's great about being in this business is that it gives you the freedom to do what you love. Whether it's gaming, social, travel or entertainment, the App industry allows you to pursue it and generate revenue 24/7/365. It is a new frontier for innovation and creating disruptive movements. We've seen many traditional industries change by using Apps such as:

- Transportation with Uber

- Hospitality with Open Table

- Housing with Airbnb

- Transactions with Square

- Photos with Instagram

- Gaming with the success of Angry Birds

App creators are the visionaries who impact hundreds of millions of people every day. They disrupt industries and, in many cases, change the world for the better.

App creators are the new celebrities. Evan Spiegel, the creator of Snapchat, married a Victoria Secret model. The creator of Minecraft reportedly bought the most expensive house in Beverly Hills living next to Leonardo DiCaprio and George Clooney.

There is no better time in history for you to begin than now.

Traditional Desktop Web Surfing is Dying

In 2014, mobile internet usage surpassed desktop usage. Having a traditional website that is not mobile optimized is an easy way to become irrelevant in today's economy.

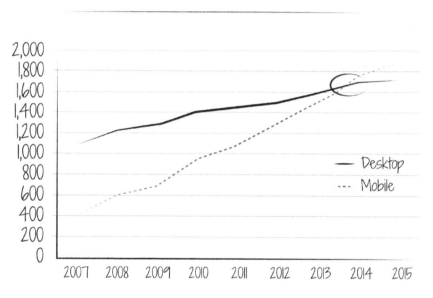

Number of Global Users (Millions)

Source: Morgan Stanley Research

The ecosystem in Silicon Valley, California has been at the forefront of the mobile movement since Apple first released the iPhone. Previously, Silicon Valley's recommended platform for a startup was to go mobile before creating a website. It was considered easier and faster to establish a Product–Market–Fit by going mobile first.

Today, the movement has shifted from mobile first, to MOBILE ONLY. I'm not saying having a website is bad, but having an App and mobile web presence is much better. Most Google searches occur today on mobile devices. Google will soon recommend engaging Apps instead of websites.

Additionally, billions of people around the world are getting Internet access for the first time in rural parts of South America, Africa, and India. Most do not own a computer so they use smartphones instead. This means a traditional website may not let you access future opportunities for your product or service.

Businesses Risk Irrelevance without a Mobile App

Traditional businesses have become more reliant on mobile users than ever before. Any retail or any online store is at a disadvantage if they are not engaging users on a mobile device. Why? Because their competitors are doing it!

Here are two examples: Starbucks, a traditional business which generates revenue from selling coffee, has more than 50-million people using their App monthly. Great Clips, a brick and mortar barber shop, has more than five million downloads of its App.

Why would a company that sells coffee and another that cuts hair need an App? Neither business sells a product or service that is directly accessible through the App. So why bother having one?

The answers are: customer engagement, brand recognition and increased sales. Retailers understand the value of an App comes in the form of mobile purchasing, reservations, keeping the customer engaged with your brand and incentivizing rewards. If you have a business and currently do not have an App, this book will show you incredible opportunities for growth.

CHAPTER 2

CREATING A
WINNING APP MINDSET

J ohn D Rockefeller became the world's first billionaire in 1916. It took 30 years for Henry Ford to become the second one. Forbes magazine reports, there are more than 1,800-billionaires currently in the world today with an estimated two new billionaires created weekly.

There has never been a faster industry in history in which to create a billion-dollar company than the App Industry. It took Instagram four years to be the first billion-dollar App. It previously took 10-12 years for traditional industrial businesses like Coca Cola and IBM to reach billion-dollar status.

As of 2017, Apple and Google have paid more than $130-billion-dollars to App creators. A new App reaches the billion-dollar valuation every six months. Will yours be next?

Mobile technology has become affordable, available, and ubiquitous to almost everyone. Today, an eight year old boy living in an African township with a smartphone has better access to information than the United States President did 20 years ago.

The App market is now growing faster than ever before with the global adoption of smartphones in developing countries. There are an estimated 4 billion new people across developing countries with access to the Internet via their smartphone for the first time. This means outside of the current market, there will be an additional 4 billion new people waiting for your new creation.

Limiting Beliefs

There are certain beliefs that shape your perception of the world. Most of our core limiting beliefs were inherited from our parents, culture and environment. They were not created on our own.

Most people are fighting limitations they adopted during childhood. For those that never went to a circus, a giant elephant is kept leashed to a very small rope attached to a tiny stake in the ground. If the elephant wanted to break free, it could easily take down an entire circus tent. Yet it doesn't. Why? Because it is limited to the beliefs it adopted when it was a baby. As a baby the small rope and stake were inescapable. After a few attempts to break free as a baby, it was programmed to be helpless. It has been stuck with the belief that the small rope and stake in the ground could stop it. So, it never tries to break free.

Speaking with App creators daily, I've found there are common limiting beliefs that many have regarding their capabilities. They see highly successful Apps and say, "Oh I can't do that, I don't have their resources," or "I don't have the expertise," or "I don't have the time or money." The most limiting one? "I don't deserve to make a million dollars."

I encourage you to consider your current limiting beliefs that were adopted by you while you were growing up. What's stopping you right now from fulfilling on your dreams? When you acknowledge that your limiting beliefs are in fact something you inherited, you can start to break free of them.

Unlimited Financial Potential

According to a survey conducted by Bankrate, 76% of Americans live paycheck to paycheck. That means 76% of people in one of the richest countries in the world can barely pay their bills. The average person believes they should plan on making the same as their peers, because that's what they believe they "deserve."

Let me ask you a question: Why do you deserve only $65,000 a year when 25-year-old Evan Spiegel, co-founder of Snapchat, makes $100,000,000 a year? It only took Evan four years to accumulate his wealth. It's time to break through the financial scarcity mindset that is programmed into many of us from birth. That mindset says that there is a limited supply of money and you deserve only a certain amount. The truth is there is no shortage of money to be earned or made.

If the economy needs more money, we simply print more of it. Did you know $8,000,000,000,000 in NEW currency was printed over the last 12 years? In case you didn't feel like counting the number of "0's", that's EIGHT TRILLION dollars.

How much of that money did you get? There is truly no limit to how much you can make with your App. You can make $500 a month or $5,000,000 a month. That's up to you to decide. As Jim Rohn said, "Your income is directly related to your philosophy, not the economy." Your financial mindset should be limitless.

In the following chapter on Money Mastery, we'll dive deeper into the strategies of how to optimally monetize (make money with) your App. I'll uncover the secrets that the top Apps use to make incredible profits and how you can utilize the same strategies for yourself.

Nothing is Impossible

A common trait 98% of billionaire App creators possess is that they embrace the fact that nothing is impossible. Impossible is not factual; it's an opinion. How many times throughout history did 'so-called experts' call something impossible, yet science eventually proved wrong? Things are impossible until someone comes along and shows us otherwise. The world is not flat.

Many though believe impossible is fact. Before 1903, science and technology showed it was impossible to fly through the air. Now, thousands of planes roam the skies daily.

It's all mindset. Impossible is just an opinion.

Many believed it was impossible to completely transform the transportation industry... until Uber did it. Many believed it was impossible to completely transform the hospitality industry... until Airbnb did it. Many believed Facebook would be the predominant social platform... until Snapchat came along.

I encourage you to consider that what you believe to be impossible could be proven otherwise in a moment's time. It could be tomorrow, next year, or 100 years from now. Success for most of App creators is 80% the psychology (mindset) of the business leader and 20% mechanics.

The Story of Burbn

Ever hear of the billion-dollar App Burbn? Most people haven't.

After graduating from Stanford University in 2006, a software engineer named Kevin Systrom got a job at Google working as a product marketing manager. He worked on programs such as Gmail, Google Docs, and Google Spreadsheets. He also worked at NextStop, a startup company that developed a travel App of the same name. It was there that he got an idea for a photo sharing check-in App called Burbn, back in 2010. Systrom quit his job to work on Burbn full-time.

Following the current market trend of location check-in Apps and the success of the App Foursquare, Burbn was originally designed as a competing location based social network. It let users check-in at various locations, gather points for spending time with friends, and post pictures of their meet-ups. Systrom secured $500,000 in funding from two prestigious venture capital firms: Baseline Ventures and Andreessen Horo-witz.

When the App finally launched, it failed miserably.

The App was too clunky. It was not intuitive enough. It lacked usability. It was then Systrom brought in a partner and executed a daring, 180-degree business pivot.

Mike Krieger, a software engineer like Systrom, joined the Burbn team. Krieger previously worked at Meebo, a popular instant messaging App, after graduation. Shortly after, he began looking to build his own product from scratch.

Despite differences in character, the partners had a great rapport from the beginning. It was the connection between Systrom and Krieger, combined with their desire for success, which drove them both towards a common goal. They'd both quit their jobs and were committed to giving it their very best to make Burbn work, even after the failed launch.

Instead of quitting the project all-together, the founders did something few App creators ever consider. They went back to the drawing board to dive deeply into the user experience. They needed to understand and discover what users liked and disliked about their App. Through this analysis, they uncovered the #1 feature users enjoyed was sharing and editing pictures. They loved using the Apps simple, beautiful filters to enhance them.

After reflection and analysis, the App took a different course. The focus of version 2.0 was its photo sharing capabilities. Burbn was stripped of all its extra features. It was left with three core items: photo sharing, photo filters, and the like button. They re-launched the App under a new name and Instagram was born.

The First Ever Billion-Dollar App

Instagram has become a worldwide phenomenon since it launched in October of 2010. There are very few people who haven't heard of it. The re-launch reached an astonishing 3.7-million users within its first few months. Today, there are more than 600-million active users of Instagram.

Systrom and Krieger saw an opportunity, took it and made it big. According to Systrom: "Other entrepreneurs use technology to solve existing problems. We looked at problems first, and then thought about how to solve them using technology:

Beauty — We added filters to make the photos look good.

Speed — Made it possible for the user to upload photos in a mere second.

Distribution — We made it easy for a single photo to be simultaneously uploaded to multiple networks."

Acquired For $1-Billion-Dollars

It's hard to appreciate how small the Silicon Valley community is and how few key players there are. Relationships are key. When Sequoia Capital valued a company with 13-employees and no revenues at $500-million-dollars, interest intensified.

In April of 2011, things really heated up for Instagram. Over the previous few months, its user base doubled to more than 30-million and the Android version was about to be launched. With that launch, they added another 5-million users overnight. On Sunday April 8th, 2011, Mark Zuckerberg alerted his board he intended to buy Instagram. The final number was $1-billion-dollars, a combination of Facebook stock and $300-million-dollars in cash.

The offer was double Sequoia Capital and Twitter's previous valuation of Instagram. The numbers of the deal were startling, but for Systrom the clincher was Instagram would operate independently within Facebook, something critically important to Systrom and his team.

Instagram's deal with Facebook was made public on April 9th, 2011. Since Systrom had closed the funding deal with Sequoia Capital before Facebook acquired Instagram, the firm received an instant return on its investment. Even though the deal had only a handshake agreement, Systrom honored it.

This was an amazing deal, not just for Systrom but for everyone who initially took a chance and invested in Instagram.

To help understand how great of a deal this was, look at the return that Andreessen Horowitz received. They invested the first $250,000-dollars in Instagram and received a return of $78-million-dollars, a 31,000% return!

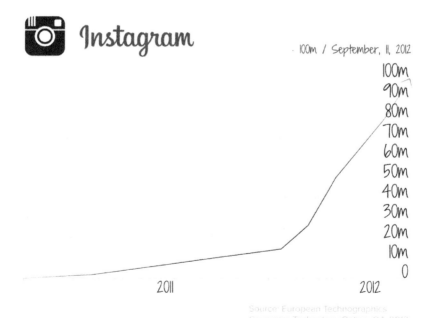

CHAPTER #3

BE A DISRUPTER

Mobile Apps have unleashed the opportunity for any business to have their products or services engage with customers unlike ever before. As a result, they have become profoundly more profitable in the process.

However, this same opportunity can cause ANY business to be disrupted. This same opportunity also leads to the extinction of entire industries faster than at any time in history. You can be the one disrupted or... the one disrupting others. As legendary business consultant Peter Drucker once said, "The best way to predict the future is to create it." If you don't continue to innovate and market your app better than others, you will probably be disrupted. Innovation and marketing are the lifeblood of any app.

Disrupting The Disruptors

My app is so disruptive
we have disruptively
disrupted other disruptors.

Use Creativity to Spot Disruptive Opportunities

Linear thinking is an evolutionary attribute. We have always thought linearly. Meaning we needed to look straight ahead to survive, capture opportunities and avoid dangers. Going back to the first days of humanity, if we failed to keep a sharp focus on our immediate surroundings, we ended up a lion's feast. Yet, what used to be good in times of danger can cripple us in times of potential.

Today, the world is much safer and, thanks to overwhelming technology growth, the world is much smaller. We are interconnected in ways unlike ever before. Digital businesses can jump from local to global in seconds. Staggering expansion contradicts linear thinking. Our natural affinity to think linearly is disrupted by the huge technological leaps we see every year.

According to a study by Ray Kurzweil, "Every twelve to eighteen months, computers double their capabilities, and so do the information technologies that use them."

Leapfrog and Disrupt an Entire Industry

Two factors separate exponential technological growth from linear thinking: disruptive stress or disruptive opportunity. At an annual event called the Genius Network, billionaire serial entrepreneur Peter Diamandis said, "there are large corporations that are stuck in linear thinking, making billion-dollar assets, and hiring hundreds of thousands of people. Then suddenly, technology comes along that displaces the need for those people. This is called disruptive stress. It's when entrepreneurs create technology that replaces the work of 1,000 people, that this is called disruptive opportunity. You can literally leapfrog an entire company that's been around for 100 years."

A great example of a company that was a market leader and had been around for 100+ years is Kodak. If you ask a millennial about Kodak, chances are they will have no idea what you're talking about. In 1976, the film giant invented the first digital camera. With that invention it created its own demise.

In 1996, Kodak had a market value of $28-billion-dollars and more than 140,000 employees. Kodak's chief engineer, Steve Sasson, invented the first digital 0.01-megapixel camera using electrical circuitry. Unfortunately for Sasson, the company's management didn't see its potential. They told Sasson it was "simply a children's toy." They were devoted to their traditional business of manufacturing chemicals and film paper.

Most of Kodak's revenue came from film. If they removed and replaced it with a digital camera, their existing multi-billion-dollar business would be in jeopardy. They owned 85 percent of the camera market in 1976.

Kodak was used to flat, linear thinking. As a result, they failed to see the potential of digital camera mass production.

The ultimate result of their linear thinking was Kodak declaring bankruptcy in 2012. Ironically, the same year the once multi-billion-dollar company that invented the digital camera went bankrupt was the year the digital photography App, Instagram, was acquired for $1 billion dollars by Facebook.

Kodak had more than 60,000 when it declared bankruptcy. At the time of its acquisition, Instagram had 13 employees. The point? Mindset differentiates a fresh entrepreneur from stagnant, long-standing market power. There are many businesses like Kodak that will be disrupted and displaced by new exponential technologies and tools.

How will you go about finding businesses that can be displaced? A great entrepreneur takes on a disruptive challenge and turns it into a disruptive opportunity. Those 'Kodaks' who create digital cameras grow rich. The 'Kodaks' who miss disruptive challenges and opportunities will disappear.

Think of it in terms of what Charles Darwin discovered, "It is not the strongest that survive, nor the most intelligent that survive. It is the one that is most adaptable to change."

Technology can suddenly replace thousands of employees. A savvy business idea jumps over several hurdles at once, replacing a multi-billion-dollar corporation in just a few years. This is the type of creative thinking that can make the difference between being the next Kodak... or the next Instagram.

The Story of Picaboo

Have you ever heard of the billion-dollar App Picaboo? If you are a millennial, there is a very good chance you use it every day, but under its re-established name Snapchat.

In April 2011, two Stanford University students forever changed the way millions of people around the world communicate. One day in a design class, Evan Spiegel presented a photo sharing App idea where the photo would automatically disappear after a period of time. The idea was dismissed by his colleagues as "silly and of very limited use." Despite the lukewarm reaction, he brought on a programmer who would become co-founder of the company, Bobby Murphy, to help him develop a prototype.

When Picaboo launched, it allowed you to take and send ephemeral pictures and instantly share them with friends. The pictures would automatically be deleted after a few seconds.

The Re-Launch

In July 2011, three months after inception, Picaboo was re-launched under its current name, Snapchat. The co-founders added enhancements to make the App more appealing to those looking to use it for texting. Snapchat has disrupted the way millennials around the world communicate.

Six years after the relaunch, Snapchat has 160-million active monthly users, 2.5-billion photos are shared daily, and the company is worth more than $8-billion-dollars. The founders have also repeatedly turned down multi-billion-dollar buyout offers from both Google and Facebook.

Snapchat has paved the way for future communication innovations and will probably continue to do so for the foreseeable future. Spiegel and Murphy understood the younger generation's need for constant communication. They acknowledged the need to feel liberated when freely sending pictures and messages, but at the same time were aware of the importance of privacy and anonymity. This was a need not being currently met with traditional social platforms such as Facebook and Twitter. Users wanted to share photos and messages without them being saved, or worse, shared to anyone other than the intended recipient.

Snapchat allows people to bond with each other in a different, more intimate way than ever before. It represents a shift in a new direction, a disruption in communication, and a progression from the desperately public way people used to communicate, to a new, safer, and more innovative way.

At a speech at the AXS Partner Summit, Evan Spiegel shared that the term "Internet Everywhere" means our old conception of the world which separated into an online and an offline space is no longer relevant. First generation social media required that we live experiences, record those experiences, and then post them online to recreate the experience and talk about it. Now, we no longer must capture the 'real world' and recreate it online – we simply live and communicate at the same time. The selfie makes sense as the fundamental unit of communication on Snapchat because it marks the transition between digital media as self-expression and digital media as communication. That's what Snapchat is all about. Talking through content, not around it. With friends, not strangers. Identity tied to now, today. Room for growth, emotional risk, expression, mistakes, room for you."

Dream Big

Many people put a limit on how big they dare to dream in life. They fail to realize imposing such a limit hurts their chance of success. If you're doing something worthwhile, you might as well do it big. It's easier to shoot for a big goal and give it everything you've got, than aim low and drag your feet over time.

Most don't give themselves permission to dream big. Go ahead. DREAM BIG! Take 10 minutes now to write down what it would look like if you had unlimited resources and nothing holding you back from making your App dream a reality. What would you create? What could you disrupt?

PART TWO

7 PILLARS OF A MULTI-MILLION DOLLAR APP

CHAPTER 4

PILLAR 1: GRAND VISION

The first pillar of the Million-Dollar App blueprint is having a clear, powerful grand vision for the future of your App business. It all starts with having a grand vision of the future. You should begin your journey with the end in mind.

You might wonder what having a clear vision has to do with creating a successful app. The reason I start these pillars with 'vision' is because I've seen creators who aimlessly launch their App without a destination or goal are the quickest to fail. I see so many people waste time and money building their App without having the end in mind. Every billion-dollar App creator at some point declared what they wanted and developed a roadmap to get there.

Begin with The End in Mind

Most people work from where they are now, to where they want to be. This is a backward strategy. You have to begin as though you already have the end in mind. As if it is already accomplished and done for you. Then work backwards, not forwards to create the roadmap to get there.

At some point, you'll go off track. It is inevitable. Whether it's developing the wrong feature, running out of money, having the wrong team or the wrong product-market-fit, you will steer off-course. It will be your grand vision for the future that puts you back on the right path. It's much easier to stay committed to your habits when there is a clear vision created.

When we are scattered and going from one thing to the next and trying a million different initiatives, it's hard to create positive results because we don't know where we're going. Mistakes are a part of doing business. If you're not making mistakes, then you're simply not innovating enough.

I sometimes go after things that inevitably may not work out. But I have a clear vision. I know what I want and where I'm going. That's the power of having a vision.

Clarity is power. You have to know the specific results you want in order to achieve them. The clearer your brain is on the target the easier it is to get there. I encourage you to get crystal clear about what you want to achieve with your App. When you don't know what you want, you will struggle. That's when we get frustrated, confused, and discouraged.

Something interesting happens to our brain when we plan. Studies show we tend to overestimate what we can do in one year and underestimate what we can do in three. Envision yourself and your App business three years from now.

Whatever that looks like for you, I believe you can achieve it. The right actions, persist over time, guarantees your success. Success won't come immediately, but with the right actions, persist over time, it guarantees that you will get there.

Create Your Vivid Vision

The first step to creating your vision is to envision yourself in the future. Cameron Herold, author of 'Double Double,' conveyed how to discover your "Vivid Vision" by first closing your eyes and then imagine yourself using a time capsule to take you 3 years into the future from today. Envision yourself sitting in your future office. Describe what you see and write it down. Describe exactly what your App business looks like.

> ➢ What type of App have you created?

> ➢ How have you impacted the lives of others?

> ➢ How many downloads do you have?

> ➢ How many people have you served?

> ➢ How much revenue has the App generated?

> ➢ How big is your team?

> ➢ What are your users saying about your App?

> ➢ What is your team saying about your App?

Once you have crafted your clear, powerful vision of what your App business will look like in the future, you can simply reverse engineer it to make it a reality. You can now put the plans and people in place to make it happen. Once you understand what you want to create and where you will be in three years, you can work backwards to figure out how you will get there. This is your map.

Think of your App business like putting together a picture puzzle. To put pieces of a puzzle together, you need a map. Your map is the picture that shows you what the puzzle looks like when it is all put together. Without the map, how do you know what the puzzle is supposed to look like? A Vivid Vision is the map for your App business. It is your end goal.

Most people work from where they are now, to where they want to be. This is a backward strategy. You have to work as though you already have the end product. As if it is already accomplished and done for you and simply work backwards, not forwards. You must be crystal clear on your vision. Focus on the value you are offering to the world. You are in control of your destiny. Now that you have a vision for the future, it's time to create specific tangible goals and the timelines to get you there.

Below are examples of billion-dollar App visions as reflected on their respective websites.

Uber – "Connect one billion people who need a reliable ride with people looking to earn money driving their car."

Square – "Revolutionizing commerce for sellers and their customers. Square creates product and services that push boundaries and innovates businesses."

Snapchat – "Improve the way people live and communicate. Our products empower people to express themselves, live in the moment, learn about the world, and have fun together."

What Is Your Desired Outcome?

I have personally failed multiple times over the years because I did not have a vision. I created and launched Apps in hopes of their being successful but I didn't have clear goals in mind.

Today, I meet more than two-dozen App creators every week. Half of them have no goals for their App. The other half have very modest goals, reaching an extra 50,000 - 100,000 downloads soon, or even making an additional $10,000 in sales a month.

As soon as you set your goals, you'll be able to act with confidence and work backwards to meet your goals. All you have to do is reverse engineer from where you want to be, to where you are right now. If you're waiting on results to believe it, then it's not going to happen.

The most successful and productive people use the 80/20 rule. 80% of your results come from 20% of your efforts. To get clear on what actions need to be taken, you must first understand your desired result. What is the outcome you want with your App? When will you achieve that outcome? Go ahead and write it down now.

Be crystal clear on the destination. The actions you take here are going to be different depending on your desired outcome. Is your goal to have a billion-dollar App in 4 years? Is it to have one million active users by next year? Or is it to make an extra $5,000 per month?

If you don't have a destination or a clear goal in mind, then how will you know what path to take? I've found that my vision becomes clearer when I am out of my normal business setting. Nature finds a way of pulling my vision out of me.

How to Get What You Want

After working with and interviewing some of the most successful App creators, what is it that these Apps have in common? What do these Apps do so consistently that makes them so successful? You might be surprised, since it's not what you would necessarily think.

They all have goals and dreams that are bigger than themselves. These goals compel them to get up every single morning and work harder and smarter than anyone else. They are motivated to be resourceful and to make their dreams a reality. They have compelling goals that are not just driven by making money. They want something more.

They are driven to be the best. They are committed and demand more of themselves than their peers; more than anyone else could expect. If you demand more from yourself than anyone else, there is no limit to what you can achieve. You'll have access to a limitless level of success and happiness in your life.

There are more than 30,000 new Apps introduced into the market every month. The majority are launched with no direction, map, or goal. The most important but often overlooked part of attaining success is setting goals to achieve it.

Why do so many people work so hard, do honest work and never achieve anything? Meanwhile it seems others don't work as hard, yet achieve great things? I have noticed those who become successful typically continue to be successful. I have also noticed those who are perceived to be failures, typically continue to fail.

It all comes down to setting goals. Having tangible goals lets you choose what you intend to make happen. Simply focusing on these goals sets the universe in motion to help you achieve them.

Goals are different than your vision. They are the steps you take to achieve your grand vision of the future.

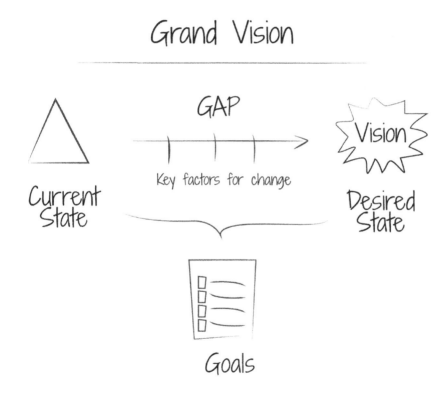

When You Visualize, You Materialize

When you visualize something vividly and frequently, it begins to manifest itself into reality. However, one thing I want to make clear is that it can't be something out of your control. For example, winning the lottery is a vision a lot of people share but it's one that's completely out of their control. Your vision must be something that can occur based on actions taken by you to get there.

Setting goals is the first step to turning the invisible into the visible. People with goals achieve because they know where they're going and have a clear direction. It's that simple.

Imagine you're on a soccer field kicking the ball around with others. But there's no goal to kick the soccer ball into. That makes it impossible to score. It's impossible to put the ball in the net, if there is no goal. If there is no goal, then you're not playing soccer. You are just kicking a ball aimlessly around a field, right?

You do the same thing in life if you don't know what it is you want to achieve. Without specific goals, you're never playing the game to begin with. And that's where most Apps fail. If you have no goal, you have nowhere to go.

You may have all of the right habits, passion, drive, and persistence, and still wonder why you haven't achieved the results or outcomes you set out for. The reason is because you're wandering without specific goals and set dates of when you'll accomplish them. It's impossible to score if you're not playing the game.

A Goal Without a Plan Is Just a Wish

Once you have your goals for your new App, it's time to create a plan to achieve it. As Ben Franklin once said, "If you fail to plan, you plan to fail." Many mistake goals as dreams or general achievements. Goals can never be general. They must be specific.

A powerful goal has five components using the acronym SMART:

Specific

Measurable

Attainable

Realistic

Timely

When your goals inspire you – when you believe and act on them – you WILL accomplish them. I create and update my 6-month, 1-year and 2-year goals regularly. They are pinned in my office and on my refrigerator at home so I see them every day.

I also share my goals with others. I suggest you do the same. What you tell others embodies how you feel and act. Right now, I want you to write down your goals so that they are given life! This one act transforms the intangible into reality. Something very powerful occurs when you write down your vision, your goals to get there and begin visualizing yourself achieving them.

Napoleon Hill, author of 'Think and Grow Rich,' said, "Goal setting and detailed planning are the basis of every achievement. Every success story begins with people who know what they want to achieve. So, before you begin chasing after any old dream, you should start by defining your own personal goal as precisely as you can. For example, if you want to get rich, you should decide precisely how much money you want to make. Additionally, you must have a clear understanding of <u>when</u> you want to achieve your goal and what you're prepared to invest to accomplish it. Because setting a specific goal is pointless if it's floating in some indeterminate future where you'll only ever be able to pursue it halfheartedly."

Vague Goals Lead to Vague Results

A goal is a very specific desired outcome, with a specific completion date and a plan of the steps needed to complete it. "I want more money", "I want more downloads" or "I need to improve retention" are not goals. Make your goals something very clear – something that inspires you. Good goals should not necessarily be easy to obtain.

As author Jim Rohn explains on Success.com, "Goal setting provides focus, shapes our dreams and gives us the ability to hone in on the exact actions we need to take to get everything in life we desire. Goals are exciting because they provide focus and aim for our lives. Goals cause us to stretch and grow in ways we never have before. To reach our goals, we must become better; we must change and grow."

Take Massive Action

When it comes to getting results and becoming wildly successful, you need to have a mindset of taking <u>massive action</u>.

Action creates reaction.

Those who take the most correct actions over a sustained period, inevitably succeed. You're going to make mistakes. It's OK. Get out of your comfort zone. As Max Depress says, "We cannot become who we want to be by remaining who and what we are."

Truly successful App creators are those who are willing to do the things today most others won't, so that they can live the life that most others can't. I'm not going to tell you success comes easily. Nor will I tell you, you can achieve it by taking mediocre actions. That's simply not true.

Most people incorrectly estimate the amount of action it takes to get the results they want. For those who don't succeed, they did not assess the amount of action needed to attain their success. There are no million-dollar ideas; there are ONLY million-dollar executions. An idea is worthless until it has been executed.

I love getting things done and I'm sure you do too. I'm happiest when I'm being creative and seeing progress. I'm sure you are the same way; otherwise you wouldn't be reading this book. As Tony Robbins often says, "Progress equals happiness."

It's satisfying to see results and you must take massive action to get there.

No Action = No Results

What a rip off.. I've been working for 3 minutes and I'm still not rich!

The amount of success you achieve is only limited by the number of actions you take and the value you offer.

Success = Actions + Value

You can take a break when you're finished and sell your App. For now, you must take massive action to achieve your goals. You must push hard and execute fast.

Do you think all the top Apps on the market took mediocre actions to get to where they are today? Of course not! Each consistently took massive action to reach their next level of success and stay at the top... so should you.

Always look for opportunities to act. Occasionally, one new action or change in direction can produce a runaway response. Think of the domino effect or a tumble weed that picks up size and speed with wind. You are looking to create that kind of energy and momentum.

The amount of luck you have is directly proportional to the number of actions you take. The more actions you take, the more luck you will have. Jim Rohn coined the familiar term, "You are the average of the five people you hang out with every day."

In reality most people spend their time with employees, family, and friends. Using this logic, your net worth is far less than what it is. I prefer what Grant Cardone says: "You are the average of the five actions you take every day."

Are you consistently taking positive, healthy actions each day that move you closer towards your goals? If you answered yes, then you're going to achieve many of your dreams.

Success Is Your Duty, Obligation, & Responsibility

You don't acquire success. It's something you create by taking massive action. Success is not a journey. It's state of mind. It's a constant state where you have complete control. It's your responsibility.

Success is fulfillment. It's about achieving something positive in your life. It must be something that's good for you and good for others. You were created to do this. It's your duty. It's a "thank you" back to the universe for giving you the unique abilities and courage that you possess.

You can create success through taking the right actions over time or continue to be average. It's that simple. I see developers repeatedly give up and stop taking the right actions. I want better for you.

For you to see extraordinary results, you must outwork and outsmart your competitors. Refuse to end your day until you have put in massive action towards your goals. Don't just stay busy, rather be busy being productive. Once you achieved some success, it's important to continue to outwork and outsmart your potential competitors. Otherwise they will catch up to and defeat you.

Average is a recipe for failure. Average is taking mediocre steps forward. No one will come to your house and make your dreams come true. It requires taking massive action and having mental domination. Do this and you'll smoke your competitors! Taking the right actions, consistently leads to inevitable, unprecedented success.

Think 10X Bigger

Now that you have your goals written down, look at ways you can achieve them in the shortest amount of time. Billionaire entrepreneur and early Facebook investor, Peter Thiel, once asked Mark Zuckerberg,

"Why can't you achieve your 10-year plan in the next 6 months? What is stopping you?"

I encourage you to ask yourself the same question.

Discover your target and multiply it by ten. Most businesses focus on improving their efforts by 10%. They ask themselves and their team, "How can we increase our sales by 10% in the next quarter?" This is thinking small. Rather than asking how you can grow 10%, ask how you can grow ten times! When you start thinking big, true breakthrough innovation comes to fruition.

Now that you have clear and defined goals in mind, I encourage you to multiply them by ten. What do your goals look like after you expanded them? Billion-dollar Apps did not reach the growth of where they are today by increasing 10% gradually over time. They each had initial goals that were later expanded by ten times. As soon as you begin to think 10 times bigger, three magical things begin to occur.

Number 1: You out create your obstacles and competitors. Even if you currently have no idea how to get to there, you'll be amazed at what happens. You must let go of the limitations of your past and let yourself run! When Elon Musk built Tesla, he started with a clean sheet of paper and imagined what could be possible.

Number 2: When you think 10X bigger rather 10% bigger, it's a hundred times the value proposition, but it's never 100 times harder or more expensive.

Number 3: 10X bigger people attract more gifted, creative and hard-working partners. Whether the need arises for a partner, an employee, a vendor, an investor... these people become more available to you simply because you're thinking bigger.

It's important to 10X your goals in order to reach a level of growth that far exceeds any other potential competitor. Take Uber for example, once the app began to reach its initial traction it had been copied hundreds of times in various cities around the world. The reason is because just like most apps, Uber's basic service was easily and cheaply replicable. Most of Uber's early competitors started with less than a million dollar investment. So in order for Uber to succeed it was critical to grow at an exponential rate in order to shut out its competition. Once you begin to reach initial traction you must do the same.

When you begin to think in the realm of 10X you'll be amazed by the capabilities you create, and what it enables you to do. There's a multitude of benefits, and payoffs, that come from expanding your mind and taking massive action. To truly achieve your goals, you must BECOME the person you want to be. Resist temptations that stand in your way and eliminate all obstacles to success by planning properly, taking the necessary actions and making decisions that will allow you to become the person you KNOW you can be!

- Key Points -

➢ When you visualize, you materialize.

➢ Begin with the end in mind.

➢ Setting goals is the first step to turning the invisible into the visible.

➢ Figure out what you want and where you want to be FIRST and then work backwards.

➢ When you think 10X bigger versus 10% bigger, you become 100X more valuable. It's never 100X more expensive, nor 100X harder.

➢ The impossible becomes possible by simply shifting your mindset.

- Action Steps -

➢ What is your vision for your App? Begin with the end in mind and the outcomes you want 3 years from now.

➢ You need to name it to claim it! What are you claiming?

➢ Create 3 simple clear goals with tangible details and outcomes. Be as detailed as possible. Be crystal clear on what they are and when you want to achieve it.

➢ What is the timeframe you will achieve your goals by?

➢ How many App downloads do you want?

➢ How many active monthly users?

➢ How much revenue per month?

What's Next?

Now that you have a vision and established goals for your App, it's time to formulate a plan for execution. Innovation and marketing are the lifeblood of any business. With more than 3-million competing Apps on the market, together we'll begin to uncover how innovation is the key to dominating others.

CHAPTER 5

PILLAR 2: INNOVATION

Innovation is the second essential pillar for building a successful App. Without it, you are a commodity. To innovate in its purest form is to solve your users' needs better than anyone on the market. It is adding superior value to the end user. The key is being user centric: knowing your users' wants and needs better than anyone else. You can innovate in many ways but it's useless if it doesn't provide a perceived advantage.

Innovation must be continuous. If you don't provide innovation based benefits on a continuous basis to your customers, you won't keep them. Your retention rate will drop as users move on.

Create Something People Simply Can't Live Without

Why do you think Square, Snapchat, Evernote, Uber, and other billion-dollar Apps launch new innovative enhancements every few months? If they don't continue to innovate they will become irrelevant in the near future.

Serial entrepreneur, Gary Vaynerchuck, once asked, "Why were Garret Camp and Travis Kalanick (founders of Uber), two people outside of the transportation business, able to create such a successful company that's putting taxi cabs out of business? How did two broke roommates, Brian Chesky and Joe Gebbia (founders of Airbnb), figure out they could rent out their San Francisco loft and start competing with Hilton? The answer was simple: they innovated where their traditional rivals didn't. They were innovators that saw the white space in the evolving internet marketplace."

Innovators Dilemma

Our App Idea
Is Like Snapchat,
Meets Airbnb,
Meets Instagram,
Meets Spotify,
Meets Something We
Haven't Even Thought Of Yet...

You Had Us At
"Like Snapchat"

Innovating How Businesses Accepts Payments

Back in 2009, a simple money problem got an entrepreneur thinking. His friend, a craftsman who sold local goods, had just lost a prospective buyer due to not being able to accept credit cards as a means of payment. Traditional credit card processing machines cost thousands of dollars back then and were very cumbersome. He asked himself the important question, 'How can we innovate the current credit card process so we can seamlessly allow anyone to accept and process credit cards from anywhere in the world?'

We all have smartphones, right? Why not turn them into credit card processing machines? With a smartphone, there was no need for any kind of expensive additional equipment. Someone comes up to you with a credit card and boom! You get paid on the fly! This new App would allow everyone to use their smartphones and tablets as portable, hassle-free credit card terminals.

Through trial and error, he began to turn his App dream into reality. Jack Dorsey, the man behind Twitter, is the co-founder of Square Inc. The company created the first ever smartphone credit card processing App. It was innovation at its purest. It solved users' needs better than anything else on the market.

Square was named after its square-shaped credit card readers, whose design was heavily praised when it was released. Many compared it to something Apple would make, clean, rectangular, and sleek.

It allows the ability to process any kind of credit card payment. Regardless of where you are, all you need is your phone, the App, and the reader which plugs into your phone's headphone jack. Square even offers the card reader and the App free of charge, allowing you to set your business up as soon as possible. There are no up-front costs and no hassle. Dorsey strategically removed all barriers and objections for any business to seamlessly use the product.

Square Inc. was valued at more than $6 billion dollars in January 2017. It has more than 3-million users worldwide, 250,000 of which are businesses or merchants. Dorsey provided a solution to a real problem, stripped away all unnecessary fluff to uncover the simplest form of innovation. In so doing, he revolutionized the merchant services sector.

What the company did was unheard of in the market at that time. They combined two things people took for granted — the use of their smartphones and ability to pay for goods or services with a credit card — and turned it into a financial platform for the future.

Continued Innovation

Square's innovations didn't stop there. In 2013, they introduced new products that complemented their original card reader: Square Stand (an iPad App that turned the device into a point-of-sale (POS) system), Square Register (a POS system that aimed to replace traditional cash registers), and Square Cash (a feature that allowed the users to send each other cash directly). There is a good chance you have used the Square Register at a coffee shop or boutique retail store as they are now prominently used around the world.

The company continues to innovate and provide the greatest value to business owners and professionals in need of an affordable, efficient mobile credit card processing tool. Since the launch of Square, there have been dozens of competing Apps introduced. So, to stay relevant, Square must continue to innovate and provide the greatest value to both businesses and consumers.

Solving a Billion-Dollar Problem

There isn't a problem in the world innovation can't solve. The quickest way to become a billionaire is to help a billion people. But how do you build a company with a worth of $1 billion dollars? The answer is, you find a $10 billion dollar or greater problem and solve it.

At a Genius Network Event, billionaire entrepreneur Naveen Jain shared, "There are three types of people who inhabit our planet. There are those who merely see the issues we face, these are called Human Beings. There are those among us who find hypothetical solutions to those issues. They are called the Visionaries. Then there are the ones who actually go out and <u>create</u> a real solution to the problem...the true Entrepreneurs!"

Jain believes: **(1)** these entrepreneurs are who create solutions to problems others can identify but fail to act upon. This includes both those who create meaningful Apps and entrepreneurs who help create the viable solutions of the future.

(2) It is no more complicated to build a company valued at $100-million-dollars than to build one valued at $1 billion dollars. Think about the impact you could have if you solved a financial, housing, transportation or educational issue for billions of people worldwide. Those are $100 billion dollar problems. Find an innovative solution to the planets' real issues and, in the process, you will become a Billionaire.

So how can <u>you</u> impact the lives of billions of people with your innovation?

How People Use Apps

Another way to look for innovative opportunities is to discover how people currently use their phones. On average, people globally spend more than 85% of the time on their smartphones using native Applications. Most of their time (84%) is spent using only five Apps. Those five Apps will vary from person-to-person. For some, their top five could include social media or gaming while others may spend more time in dating or shopping.

When you think about these new opportunities, you need to understand it's never about creating something that is going to add to the amount of time people spend on their phone. It's about replacing time spent on existing Apps.

Here is where people spend the most time within Apps by category.

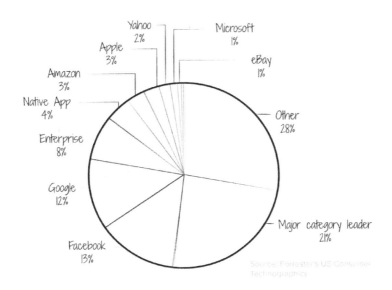

Share Of Minutes Spent On Apps Owned By Major Tech Companies

Yahoo 2%
Microsoft 1%
Apple 3%
eBay 1%
Amazon 3%
Native App 4%
Other 28%
Enterprise 8%
Google 12%
Major category leader 21%
Facebook 13%

Source: Forrester's US Consumer Technographics

Breakthrough Innovation

Sometimes the smallest positive change results in the greatest impact. A single small enhancement can have a breakthrough impact and become the greatest innovation. You don't need to reinvent the wheel or be the first to market to succeed.

In fact it's best to emulate what is currently working in the market and add or improve upon it. Evernote was not the first list building productivity app. Uber was not the first ride-sharing app. Snapchat was not the first social app. They all simply emulated what worked and innovated in a way that solved users' needs better than any other on the market.

Although not originally an App, one great example is YouTube. YouTube is now the 2nd most popular website in the world with more than 5-billion video views every single day. Contrary to popular belief, YouTube was not the first social video platform. Vimeo was first to market. They had a 1-year lead. The creator of YouTube, Chad Hurley, modeled Vimeo and did essentially the same thing, only better.

YouTube was practically identical. But the difference is YouTube was sold for $1.65-billion-dollars while Vimeo was worth around $100-million-dollars. You might be surprised to learn that the $1.65 billion dollar difference was not efficiency, speed, or quality. The greatest attribute to YouTube's growth was the Share button. At the time, Vimeo had 1 option to share a video that you were watching, while YouTube had 9 different share options.

YouTube was also among the first to use Flash video while Vimeo used QuickTime. YouTube's sharing through Flash integrated with MySpace and many other popular websites which provided an incredible early distribution advantage. Although Vimeo was first, YouTube took advantage of the proven market and what people wanted.

They innovated their platform to make videos more accessible, shareable, and leveraged distribution channels. Can you think of an App with great potential that you can enhance (or simplify) to have a greater advantage? Successful App ideas are all about looking for new or unusual combinations of other existing ideas.

What do people "WANT" and "NEED"

What is the single worst decision you can make with your App? The answer: building an App that no one wants. One of the biggest mistakes that App creators make is falling so in love with their own product that they miss out on what users actually want.

There is a misconception I have found which wastes App creators' time and money. They spend months (sometimes years) building an App they believe people "need." The problem with that method is because someone "needs" something, it doesn't necessarily mean they 'want' it. For example, most people in the United States 'need' to lose weight. But do they? People 'need' to make more money. But do they? People 'need' to floss their teeth every day. But do they? There are a lot of things people 'need' to do, but don't. Not because it's hard for them. They simply don't want to.

So ask yourself, why would they 'want' your App? It must always come down to what your users 'want.' Do everything in your power to understand what they 'want.' Learn what their desired result is.

In a world of constant change, you should fall in love with your customer (not the product) and continue to provide the best value on the market. You could be your App's #1 fan and love everything about it. But if your customers don't 'want' it, it will become irrelevant very quickly.

If you care enough about the solution you provide and are creative enough, there is no limit to what you can build. Fall in love with serving your customers' wants and needs. Successful innovation requires you to become obsessed with solving your customer's needs in a new and better way.

It's important to fully understand what your customers want, what they need and what they fear. If you do what everyone else does but a little bit better, you'll have a slight advantage. If you do what no one else does, you'll have an enormous advantage.

What Incredible Customer Experience Can You Create?

To best leverage technology to create an App people actualy want, it's important to consider the user experience. Creating the App and then figuring out how to market it later, is NOT a best practice. Most Apps are created just because the founders thought it was such an ingenious idea. So, they built a prototype, spent months refining and creating the actual App, only to discover users don't want it.

At the Worldwide Developer Conference in 1995, Steve Jobs shared a profound statement about how Apple creates products, "What I have found is you have to start with the customer experience and work backwards with the technology. Not the other way around. You can't create the technology, and then try to figure out how to sell it. As we came up with the vision and the strategy for Apple, it started with what incredible benefits and experience can we give the customer. We did not sit down with the engineers and figure out what awesome technology we have, and how we can market it."

I can't stress enough how important it is to build your product around the audience you serve. When meeting with dozens of App creators each week, I've found most people define their App by the product or service they sell, rather than the audience they serve. So many creators build their App believing if they have great features, people will automatically love it. Too many App creators fall into the trap of creating and building Apps with hundreds of features they believe users want.

This is what they call the "if you build it, they will come" philosophy. But if you're not a user centric App business, then you will struggle to remain relevant in the future. Tony Robbins once said, "You have to really spend as much time 'on' your business as you do 'in' your business." Meaning before you get lost in development, technology, and features, it is critical to fully understand who you are creating the App for and whether they will enjoy it.

Two years later in 1997 at the Worldwide Developer Conference, Steve Jobs said, "At Apple we always start at the psychology and then we figure out the technology. We start at discovering what people want, and then find the most beautiful and simplistic way to provide it. Then step two is to actually figure out the way to build it."

Since he created the App Industry, wouldn't it be wise to follow Jobs' advice with your own App?

Those who fall in love with their products eventually disconnect from the needs of their customers. Think about Facebook versus Twitter. While Twitter has struggled to grow as a dominant social media platform, Facebook continues to innovate, reinvent itself and jump to the next place their customers want to be – from desktop to mobile, to video and now into virtual reality.

Facebook anticipates the future needs of their customers and ensures these needs are served both now and in the future. You should do the same if you want to succeed. You need to define your business based on who you serve, rather than base it on what you do. This is a major difference that will lead to your success or failure in the mobile App industry.

Pivot Until You Find Your Product – Market – Fit

In the book 'The Lean Startup', Eric Ries explains the first step to creating a product people want is by starting with a "minimum viable product" and improving it based on user feedback. This is contrary to what most App creators do. They usually launch with what they believe is their perfect final product.

Most extraordinary Apps are the result of one or more major pivots. What most people don't know is that WhatsApp, Uber, Airbnb, and Snapchat were successful because of a major pivot in their business. This means their original idea for these billion dollar apps didn't work. So, they decided to evolve and move that idea in another direction. They continued to test and pivot until they discovered their Product-Market-Fit. In order to reach Product-Market-Fit your app must be a viable, valuable and validated.

Mark Zuckerberg once said, "In a world that's changing really quickly, the only strategy that is guaranteed to fail is not taking risks."

Don't Forget About Product-Market-Fit

As the creator, it is your job to decide when it's the appropriate time to evolve your idea. You must continue to pivot until you reach your Product-Market-Fit and hit critical mass. When you think you're working on something and you feel you have failed, that failure can ironically turn out to be the recipe for your next big success.

Consider Airbnb, an App that is now valued at more than $30 billion dollars. What most don't know is that the original concept for Airbnb failed in 2007. Back then, co-founders Joe Gebbia, Brian Chesky, and Nathan Blecharczyk, originally named the service Air Bed and Breakfast. It was designed as a cheap service that offered air beds in apartments for people attending conferences to sleep upon. The service was only designed for that purpose. They offered breakfast and the opportunity to network with fellow guests of that conference.

The co-founders could have spent their money and energy trying to force this original idea and possibly create a small niche business. Instead, they treated the service as something fluid. They improved it based on what they discovered their customers wanted. They continued to think bigger until they served millions of people who loved it! Everything they did was based on user feedback and App usage patterns. They adapted based on what users wanted.

They shortened the name from Air Bed and Breakfast to Airbnb and abandoned the complicated breakfast networking part of the business. They redefined the service as a simple and easy to use place for people to rent any type of housing imaginable. Airbnb listings include houses, castles, apartments, penthouses, and even entire private islands. They went from being in the 'cheap bed' business to being in the creating global adventures business.

From Status Update App To Instant Messaging

After two decades working at the same place, two highly esteemed IT professionals (Jan Koum and Brian Acton) at Yahoo! were quickly reaching a saturation point in their jobs. They agreed that it was time to make a career change. Their new professional paradigm was "Let's make people's lives just a little bit better."

They started their own company and built a "status" update App. The idea originally came from Koum who wanted to let everybody know that he was busy at the gym. That iteration of the App didn't work at all. Very few people gave it a second look. It failed.

At one point, Koum wanted to quit and look for a regular job, but Acton, the financier and co-founder, managed to discourage him from leaving the startup. It was only after a couple of his friends back home in the Ukraine told them about how they'd like to be able to message him in the United States for free and not pay 30 or 40 cents per message. Based on this feedback they started thinking about adding a messaging feature. That's when the outline of the new app started to take shape.

Koum and Acton are the brains behind the App known as WhatsApp. WhatsApp exploded across the globe. A couple of career software engineers were elevated to multi-billionaire industry leaders. A few years later, Facebook acquired WhatsApp for $19 billion dollars, making it the biggest mobile App acquisition in history.

If they continued with the original status update App idea, they would have inevitably run out of both time and money. Instead, WhatsApp evolved based on their users' desire of offering free messaging. It shifted because of a simple feature, instant messaging.

WhatsApp has more than 1 billion monthly users. It allows people all over the world to send messages at no cost. It also lets users speak internationally with each other and in groups at no cost over VoIP and Wi-Fi.

As of this writing, WhatsApp remains the most iconic and preferred global Application for instant text messaging. Whatever your current App idea may be, stay open to pivoting based on user feedback if you truly want to succeed.

How to Get to Product-Market-Fit

The first step to getting to your Product-Market-Fit is to have the humility to continually alter your product based on your users' engagement and feedback. When first launching the App Evernote back in 2008, the co-founders placed their initial budget on Product Development to create the best organizing App on the market. Although this meant initial growth would be slow, it paid off in the end.

Evernote is now one of the top productivity Apps on the market, valued at more than $1 billion dollars. Evernote's founder Phil Libin once stated, "People who are thinking about things other than making the best product, never make the best product." I encourage you to consider your best step may be improving your App to ensure it's **remarkable.**

Create a User Centric App

Don't waste your time creating a copycat App, cloning an existing App or creating an App with no value. Instead of directly copying an App, model its success. How we spend our time daily reflects who we are, so why not choose to create something amazing?

The world doesn't need another shitty, poor quality App. There are millions of shitty, poor quality Apps already on the market. Every so often, Apple eliminates them all from the App Store to never be seen again.

With millions of Apps currently on the market, there are many that may offer a similar solution to yours. Your best differentiator is the experience you offer your users. This major difference will lead to success or failure. As American poet Maya Angelou once beautifully stated, "People may not remember exactly what you did, or what you said, but they will always remember how you made them feel."

A great example is Tinder vs. Bumble. Both Tinder and Bumble are social dating Apps. Each is worth more than $1 billion dollars. While both provide the same exact solution, matching people together for dates, the difference is in the user experience. Tinder's experience is geared towards a male user while Bumble is geared more towards a female user.

People are loyal to the experience, not the product. A recent survey by Defaqto states, "55% of consumers have reported that they would pay more for a better customer experience."

Carlos Angel, Marketing Manager at Uber, describes Customer Experience or (CX) as, "the perpetual optimization of customer value and success through data driven marketing activities."

Uber has established customer's confidence and dominates other ride sharing Apps because they provide a better experience by offering more available cars and getting the user to their destination faster and easier than other ride sharing options.

What Do People Want?

After analyzing thousands of apps I have found three human needs that drive the greatest demand for an app. If you can satisfy one or more of these needs, you will find the sweet spot to creating an innovative and highly profitable App.

1. APPEARANCE & HEALTH

Human beings are obsessed with themselves. People care about their health and appearance, which mean that they are willing to pay to enhance it. If your App can make someone feel or look better (either to themselves or their peers), your App will be incredibly valuable. Great examples of this category would be health Apps like Fitbit or social networking Apps like Facebook and Instagram that allow you to be admired by your friends.

2. MONEY

The most sought after intangible human need is money. If you can create something that helps saves money or makes someone money, you are on the right track. Great examples are finance tracking Apps like Mint or ecommerce Apps like Amazon or Poshmark that allow people to make money by selling products.

3. TIME

Lastly, what do the all-time most successful billion-dollar Apps like Uber, Airbnb, and Evernote have in common? They all sell – time. If your App saves users time, people will massively overpay you for it. Time is arguably the easiest human need to solve. Uber saves time getting a taxi.

People today seek instant gratification. Think about the last time you were upset when the app you were using was delayed, taking seconds or minutes longer than it should. If products are faster and more convenient, they will be perceived as valuable. Users pay a premium for time. It is no coincidence that Apps such as Uber and Airbnb have developed into billion-dollar companies, because these Apps save users both time and money.

Exceptions to the Rules

Two prime examples are: gaming and entertainment Apps. If you entertain users via a game or some other method, you can still solve a need and develop a billion-dollar App as we have seen with Angry Birds, Candy Crush and Clash of Clans. These Apps follow slightly different principles:

Simple — Used and loved by all ages.

Social — Incorporate mechanisms that encourage social engagement between 2 or more people.

Addictive — Attributes that compel users to use the App multiple times a day.

The greater the value and impact your App has on others, the more downloads and revenue it will receive. With these human needs in mind, consider how your App can better incorporate them.

Take Airbnb for example. Renting out people's homes and apartments was not a new idea. HomeAway was founded 3 years before Airbnb, offering the same service and was a multi-billion-dollar company until Airbnb began to dominate the market. How did Airbnb overtake HomeAway and become five times more valuable offering the same service? Airbnb didn't offer anything different. Both companies offered the same service of renting out vacation properties. The difference was in how HomeAway marketed themselves. They offered vacation rental properties and the option of renting out your home, which to many is a confusing concept.

The difference came down to the marketing, messaging and execution. For consumers, Airbnb marketed themselves as being cheaper and a better experience than staying at a hotel. For the renter, it was marketed as an easy way to make additional money with your spare home or bedroom if you aren't using it.

The best marketed App will always win at first, but for it to sustain growth, it must also continuously innovate. It must consistently provide the best product AND the best marketing.

The App Adoption Curve

The end goal for any App is to reach mass adoption within its target market and establish itself as market leader in its category. To reach critical mass, it's important to understand the technology adoption curve and stages of Diffusion of Innovation. This chart demonstrates the different technology adoption curve stages your App must go through to reach critical mass.

App Adoption Curve

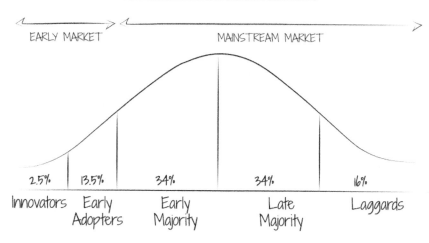

Innovators

Innovators are those aggressively looking for the newest, latest technology. Regardless of the function, these people want the next best thing to come on the market. This group is the easiest to persuade to try your App.

Early Adopters

Early Adopters buy into a new App very early in its life cycle. They appreciate the benefits of testing new technology. The members of this group are influential and give credibility to the product. Forgiveness is typically a part of their nature, so they are willing to take an imperfect product, provide feedback and help you with corrections along the way.

Early Majority

The Early Majority look for practicality. They realize many new offerings end up as fads. They are content to wait and see what others think before they buy your App themselves. This group relies on the comments and confidence of others, before they spring into buying.

Late Majority

The Late Majority waits for a new App to become established. Even after the App is known, these people need support. So, they tend to only buy from well-established companies.

Laggards

The Laggards simply are not interested in the newest thing. What they already use is fine with them. These people do not buy the next version of a phone, tablet or social media platform. It's typically a waste to market to them until you have dominated the Late Majority.

The transition between these groups is not seamless, so strategies are needed to cross over chasms that could essentially swallow up your App before it gets to the next tribe. Geoffrey Moore shares strategies to help marketers cross the cracks between groups in his book, 'Crossing the Chasm.'

Moore says in each stage, tribes are formed and they will get the population excited to the next larger stage. Once the tribes are formed, the marketer must saturate them until what is being shared spills over into the next stage.

If a new App business focuses on marketing to the Late Majority first and the product has flaws, your chance of success is minimal because the Late Majority won't deal with a product that needs adaptations. It is the early adopters who love to try anything, provide feedback along the way, look for App updates and have patience until the bugs are worked out. If an App does not target groups in order, the chance for mass adoption is dim.

Get Creative

A core differentiator between those that succeed and those that fail is that successful people continue to innovate and grow and try new initiatives, while the others do not. Those that fail continue to do more of the same initiatives (marketing, development, etc.) that aren't working. If you want to grow and reach enormous success then continually take new innovative actions forward. As Albert Einstein says, "The same level of thinking that has created your problem, won't solve your problem." You can't expect to get different results doing the same thing. If you out create your problem you will get better results every time.

When it comes to innovation, I encourage you to unleash your inner creativity. Creativity is an act of discovery. It is the process of understanding what currently works in the market (existing million-dollar Apps) and understanding what the market truly wants. As legendary copywriter George Lois writes in his book, 'Damn Good Advice,' "creativity is not created, it is there for us to find - it is an act of discovery. So, if you're trying to achieve greatness in any creative industry, go out into the world, sail the ocean blue and live a life of discovery."

- Key Points -

➢ It all starts with having a grand vision of the future and beginning with the end in mind.

➢ Sometimes the smallest innovation can result in the greatest impact.

➢ The greater the value and impact your App has on others, the more downloads and revenue it will receive.

➢ One of the biggest mistakes App creators make is falling in love with their product and not their customers. Don't make the same mistake!

➢ The best marketed App will always win at first, but for it to sustain growth and market share, it must continuously innovate.

➢ "In a world that's changing very quickly, the only strategy that is guaranteed to fail is not taking risks" - Mark Zuckerberg.

- Action Steps -

➢ If any type of technology was possible and you had an unlimited budget, what would you create?

➢ What impact do you want to make on others? Do you want to make them laugh, connect, love, or help them be more productive?

➢ What will be your WOW EFFECT? How will you make your users say, "WOW THAT'S AMAZING"?

➢ Get feedback and ask your customers the following critical questions: What is it that brought you to this App? What is missing from the App?

➢ What is your favorite feature of the App?

➢ What holds you back from sharing this App with others?

What's Next?

The most innovative product or service doesn't always win. You could have the most innovative product on the market and still fail to compete against your competitor. The reason is because your competitor is utilizing the power of marketing better than you are. You can't add value until your users see and appreciate what you can provide them. It doesn't matter what product you offer or what industry you are in, effective marketing is essential to success.

CHAPTER 6

PILLAR 3: GROWTH MARKETING

I n my opinion, growth marketing is two things. (1) It is the process of driving your users to your App to download and purchase what you are offering, while increasing the appreciation of your App in the process. (2) It is the continual education of your users to the advantages, benefits, and results your App brings them that no one else provides. It's about conveying how your App is both unique and irresistible.

Contrary to what most believe, just building and launching an App in the App Store doesn't mean people will naturally discover and download it. More than 3,000 new Apps are introduced daily. The chances of your App being discovered WITHOUT effective marketing...is slim to none.

Apps don't fail because they didn't build the right App. They fail because they can't get traction. Acquiring users takes creative thinking and strategic planning. Unfortunately, the old saying "If you build it, they will come" doesn't apply in the mobile App industry.

When you market correctly, convincing users to download your App becomes organic. Effective marketing does your selling in advance, so that by the time consumers come to your App, they are pre-interested, pre-motivated, pre-qualified and pre-disposed to download your App instantly.

If You Build It They Will Come Fallacy

The biggest mistake Apps make when trying to grow is failing to pursue traction while developing the App. Many developers think if you build a great App, users will beat a path to their door. Traction and product development are of equal importance. Each should get half of your attention. Experts call this the 50% rule. Spend 50% of your time on the product and 50% on growth.

When it comes to marketing, many developers feel hesitant promoting it at first because they believe their App may not be "good enough." They are afraid of what others will say about their creation, their baby. Does this sound like you? If so, by not marketing your App, you are robbing others from the potential value you can offer them with your creation. You do everyone involved a disservice by not sharing it with the world.

As business consultant, Jay Abraham, once said, "If you believe in the product or service you are selling, then you have a moral obligation to do everything in your power to get your product or service in the face of your potential customers".

Market to What People Want, Give Them What They Need

Occasionally, I teach a class on App marketing called 'How to Get an Extra 100,000 Downloads In 30 Days, WITHOUT Spending Any Money on Ads.' One of the questions I like to ask my students is, "If you and I both had built a new ride sharing App like Uber and we were in a contest to see who would get the most downloads and active users, what advantages would you most like to have on your side?"

The answers vary. Some want the advantage of offering superior cars to pick up people in, like Lamborghini or Ferraris. Others say they want to have the most beautifully designed and efficient App. Some want to be able to offer the lowest prices, like unlimited rides for only $50.

After my students finish sharing the advantages they would like to have, I reply, "Okay, I will give you every single advantage you asked for. In return, I only want one advantage. If you will give it to me, I will dominate all of you when it comes to selling rides."

So what advantage do I want? The only advantage I want is "A DESPERATE crowd who are in an immediate need to get somewhere without a car!"

Even if you have the best, most beautiful, efficient, and affordable solution, you will struggle if you can't reach those that want your solution. The best advantage is to have your product readily available to a starving market that WANTS your solution (no matter how simple that solution may be).

The truth is that if you can't get your product to your target market, everything else is pointless. You must be on the radar of groups of people who have demonstrated they are hungry for your product. This is your true target market.

How do you measure this hunger for your product? The ideal target markets are those who recently purchased a similar product to yours and have done so repeatedly. The three ideal guidelines are: buyers, timeliness, and frequency.

Buyer - A person who recently purchased a similar product (in our previous example someone who used Uber before). Naturally, groups of people who previously purchased a similar product are far more valuable than those that haven't. They have shown that they are willing to pay for the solution.

Timeliness - The more recent a person purchased something like what you offer, the more receptive they will be to your App. Get them... while they're hot!

Frequency - The more frequently someone buys a product, the higher their need is for that solution. Get them... while they're still addicted.

If you'd like to attend the next workshop for free simply go to www.AppMarketingAcademy.com/Workshop.

Understand Your Users

Marketing is about human behavior and applied psychology. If you can understand why your users do what they do, and know them better than anyone else, you can provide them with the perfect solution that meets their needs better than anyone else. People are programmed to buy and use the app that they can understand and relate to the fastest. Robert Collier, author of 'Riches in Your Reach,' wrote that to understand your users, "You want to enter the conversation that is existing in your prospect's mind."

What are they thinking about? What are their concerns and objections? What are their desires? What are their fears?

Marketing today is both easier and harder than it has ever been. It's easier because it's cheaper to market to millions of prospects with multiple platforms to engage them with. It's harder because there is so much competition. Everyone is fighting for your potential customer's attention.

In the late 1990's, marketing expert Dr. Jeffrey Lant coined the phrase, 'Rule of Seven.' He believed the average person needed to have seven interactions with your product before engaging with it. This meant it took seven exposures of an advertisement, PR mentions or sales promotional for a customer to make a purchase. In today's market, it's now estimated that it takes an average of 16 exposures to penetrate the buyer's consciousness and drive them to take action.

The problem in today's competitive environment is simply spending money on more advertisements isn't enough. You must penetrate their interest by being creative, authentic, and simple to understand. You must provide more value in your marketing than others who offer similar products or services.

The key to growth marketing is to find your target market first. Only then can you fully understand them. The more you understand their needs, the better you can connect with them and the easier it becomes to drive them to download your App.

Have the Right Message

According to Inc.com in 2005, "On average, Americans are subject to some 3,000 essentially random pitches per day." Think about your day yesterday and how many Facebook ads you saw browsing your news-feed. You probably saw Google ads in your search, sponsorships during your favorite podcast episode, billboards while driving or commercials while watching television.

You have become numb to most of these since very few commercial messages have any appreciable impact. In today's online world people are downing in information but starving for wisdom. If your marketing materials don't stand out and leave an impact, you will simply get lost in the sea of messages your prospective users ignore each day.

When it comes to downloading and purchasing Apps, people don't download or purchase out of necessity. They download and purchase based on EMOTION. Just like ANY purchase people make, they buy from emotion first. They later justify the purchase with logic.

Think about the last purchase you made? Did you buy that new pair of shoes because you needed protection for your feet? Or did you buy them because of how they made you feel? People pay for the emotional feeling that comes with that new product or service.

Apps are no different. Studies have shown that people choose using the App Uber over Lyft because of the symbolic identity of Uber.

What comes to mind when you think of Uber? Convenience? What comes to mind when you think of Candy Crush? Addicting? This is the power of messaging. What message do you want your potential users to receive? Do you want to send a message of cheap, ugly, and confusing (like most Apps on the market that make less than $500 a year)? Or would you prefer sleek, simple, fun, and exciting?

What's the difference between a $1 Bill and a $100 Bill? They both have the exact same weight, paper, size, color and type of ink. The only difference between a $1 Bill and a $100 Bill is the message on the paper. Which piece of paper would you rather have?

Do you want to present your App as a $1 App or $1,000,000 App? The difference is in your message. Simple tweaks to your message can make the difference between success and failure. It can turn a struggling App into a billion-dollar App. Will you position your App as the leader in your market, or simply just like the thousands available in your category?

Dealing with Competition

People today don't want the same thing they wanted yesterday. Although the features and solutions may be similar, the market is always grasping for a fresh new approach. As of 2017, there are over 500,000,000 people searching for new apps on the App Store every single week.

Every day, I hear from someone who believes their idea is the most unique, original, and revolutionary App on the market. They honestly believe there is nothing like it on the market. There is a good chance whatever App idea you have, there are hundreds, if not thousands of similar Apps that solve a similar problem.

Don't let that stop you from creating something unique. If something already exists and has proven to be successful, it means users' needs have been met. It means the Product-Market-Fit has already been proven. Proven products can always be improved upon!

Features vs. Benefits

A common trait among failed and dying Apps is that their marketing messaging was based on the App's features. The truth is people don't care about the features of an App. They care about benefits. They care about how the App applies to them and their life.

Let's say you created a To-Do List App. The first thing most App creators do is share the many features of what the App does. They say things like "better organize your thoughts." This is the same message thousands of other To-Do List Apps share.

Why not label your App: "The #1 To-Do List App on The Market"? Make sure that message is clearly presented at the beginning of your description, the text on your first screenshot, in your video and that your press materials have the same message. You are the market's best. People are attracted to the best, not something that is slightly better or has hundreds of features.

Articulate how the features of your App become beneficial and how it will get them to a desired outcome. Give them the feeling of that benefit. From feeling accomplished by getting more things done with a productivity App, feeling more connected and loved with your social networking App or more entertained with your gaming App.

People don't pay for features. They pay for outcomes. People buy and download Apps based on emotion that they later justify with logic. Connect with them on an emotional level and your download conversion rate will skyrocket.

How People Download Apps

In order to market your app successfully you must understand where people currently discover and download apps by each source. This way you can market to the right source and not waste your time and money marketing to the wrong one. According to a study conducted by Apptentive in 2012, the following chart shows a breakdown of how people discover and download Apps by source. 63% of all Apps are discovered and downloaded by searching the App Store and Google Play. The least downloaded source is reading a blog with 7% of downloads. If you can fully understand where users discover Apps, you can better focus your efforts on the sources that will drive the most downloads.

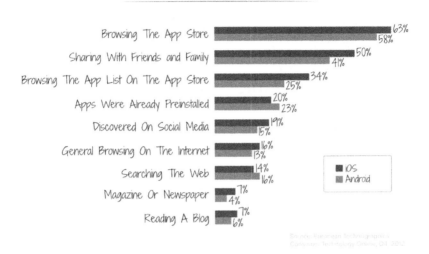

There's No Need to Reinvent the Wheel

Throughout this book, my goal is to help you avoid pitfalls that cost you both time and money following the wrong marketing method. Many new App creators try to reinvent the wheel and fail. There are marketing methods that work, and there are methods that don't. There is no need to try new methods if existing ones have already proven to be successful.

Do you think it would be wise for a new commercial airplane pilot to fly a plane filled with 100 passengers and try out new aerodynamics? What would happen if he shifted the plane up and down at different speeds and altitudes than what have worked in the past? Why would you do the same with your App?

There are fundamental marketing strategies that work that all the top Apps incorporate. If you incorporate them correctly, they will work for you too and allow you to reach a profound level of growth.

When it comes to marketing, there are two fundamental ways to get users to download your App, Organic Traffic or Paid Traffic.

Method #1: Organic Traffic

Organic Traffic includes traffic you do not own or directly control such as App Store Traffic, Social Media, Press, Apple/Google Feature, Referral Systems and any other channel that naturally drives users to your App that you do not directly pay for.

The reason you don't control this type of traffic is because you are not paying directly for advertisements or installs. For example, you don't own the Apple App Store and therefore, cannot directly drive users to your App. Organic Traffic is the most sought-after traffic since it is the most affordable method to drive the highest engaged loyal users. Any App that ever went viral was a by-product of Organic Traffic. For an App just starting out, managing and growing Organic Traffic should be your primary focus.

How to Be Found on The App Store

With 500,000,000 visitors a week, the App Store has the power to drive more than 100,000 organic free downloads a day to your App (like Candy Crush), or 0 a day (like so many). It is highly dependent on the ranking and exposure your App has on the App Store (called App Store Optimization).

PILLAR 3: GROWTH MARKETING

Think of App Store Optimization (ASO) as the way in which people naturally discover and download your App. For example, if users want an App to make their photos look better, they will search the App Store for "photo editor" and then download one of the top Apps that appear.

As shown in the previous chart, 63% of all downloads come directly from the App Store and Google Play. This makes ASO the #1 organic marketing source that drives most App downloads on the market. The depth and degree to which you master App Store Optimization, dictates your success.

Unfortunately, 90% of Apps on the market are doomed for failure because they are undiscoverable (ranked below #50 in search results). They don't incorporate effective ASO techniques. I don't want that to happen to you.

The following techniques are proven ways top Apps have been able to beat the system and reach more than 1,000 organic App downloads every day using App Store Optimization.

The "Skyrocket Method"

At PreApps, we have coined the term the "Skyrocket Method." This incorporates a strategic results-oriented organic launch strategy that has proven to 'Skyrocket' downloads and exposure with organic traffic.

I'm about to share that method with you. What follows is a breakdown of our 10-step system that is used to launch or update ANY App successfully to maximize downloads on the App Store and Google Play.

It's important to note these steps do not need to be followed in any particular order, as long as you use each of them in your launch. Think of each step as an instrument within an orchestra. Your job is to play each instrument to the best of your abilities. Every instrument is essential in the context of the symphony. You might not excel at every instrument but the app market isn't an individual performance. It's important to improve and refine each instrument to play in universal harmony for the long term.

The "Skyrocket Method"

Step #1: Creative & Searchable Name

What the top Apps understand is that the keywords you incorporate in your title are the <u>primary way the App will be discovered</u>. For example, when working with the new social networking App TagFi, we got it to #1 on the App Store for multiple keywords including "Social Group." Instead of just using the name "TagFi" we changed it to "TagFi – Social Group" As result, it outranked billion-dollar Apps like Facebook, Tango, and Google Hangouts by including strategic keywords within the App title.

When naming your App, conduct research to find the best keywords to incorporate. The keywords you select for your title have the highest-ranking weight in the App Store. We recommend limiting yourself to using your top 2 - 3 keywords in your title. Think quality over quantity. This is why the Gmail App (with more than 3-billion downloads), has the title "Gmail – email by Google; secure, fast & organized."

The structure of the Gmail titles allows the App to rank at the top of the search results for the search terms "email by Google," "fast & organized," and "fast email." Keep in mind that you may need to update and change your App name at times based on your ranking in the App Store.

The App's name should give users an impression of what it does and create an interest in learning more. Make sure your name is catchy, engaging, and descriptive.

Step #2: Eye-Catching Icon

Since the first impression a user will have of your App is the icon, it is critical you spend time making it unique, compelling and simple. A noteworthy icon uses vibrant colors and a distinctly recognizable symbol.

Instagram is a great example. It uses a symbol that is relevant to the App's name. It is also important to avoid including large amounts of text, shapes, and colors in your icon. Those elements will overwhelm users. Furthermore, they won't be noticeable on a small screen.

Consider why someone would click and select your icon over similar ones in your category. Line up five similar competing Apps and ask yourself, why would users select yours over another's? What can you do to stand out? The biggest factor is the color palette you choose to use to stand out, capture and captivate their attention.

Choose colors that will automatically create a positive association for your App. For example, blue is a good choice for a shopping App. Consumers associate blue with trust and confidence. It's no surprise that Amazon and Wal-Mart have a signature blue. Yellow is a good choice for lifestyle Apps because people associate yellow with happiness.

Step #3: Specific & Searchable Keywords

Choosing the right keywords for your app can be the difference between getting 10 downloads or 1,000 downloads a day. By working with thousands of App creators, I have found the average creator doesn't fully understand the importance of keywords. They either mistakenly choose the wrong ones or omit them all together. If you had a website and wanted to it to appear on the first page of Google when searching for it, you would incorporate specific keywords on your website. This is so Google can find and identify what your website does and send traffic to it. The same holds true for the App Store and Google Play.

Think of the App Store and Google Play as their own search engines which get more than 500,000,000 new visitors per week. When people are looking for new Apps, they go to the search bar and type in a specific search phrase to find a certain type of App.

Statistically, keyword searches are responsible for most of all App downloads. Finding the right keywords involves researching what your users naturally search for and which words your competitors use. It is important to look for keywords that have a <u>high search volume</u>, <u>low competition</u> and a <u>high probability</u> of ranking.

Research and understand the terms people naturally enter in the App Store and Google Play search bars to find the solution you offer. How many people search for that term in a month? How many other Apps are ranking for that search term?

The App Store allows you to submit up to 100-characters to rank. Take full advantage of this limit. It will allow you to have more ways for users to discover your App. There are also techniques you can use to maximize the 100 characters you have. For example, use singular forms of words instead of plural and don't spell out numbers (use 5 instead of five). The Google Play Store does not allow you to directly submit keywords. Instead, it takes ALL of your App information into consideration – your title, publisher name, description, and user reviews. Furthermore, you should change keywords in response to changes in the market.

Step #4: Viral Videos

If you want your App to go viral, you need a viral video. To give you an example, at our agency PreApps, we produced a high-quality App promo video for a new Groupon competing App called Planet Peeps, which instantly went viral reaching more than 100,000 views in just 10 days on YouTube. This is the power of having a high quality promotional video. According to the analytics agency, AdColony, 98% of the top Apps rely exclusively on video as their primary method for user acquisition. This means that the top apps on the market are using videos on the App Store, Google Play, Facebook, and YouTube to drive downloads.

In today's market videos are something your prospective users will expect. So without effective high-quality videos, your App will be at a significant disadvantage. Experts agree users are more likely to view your video than they are to go through your screenshots or read your description. So, it is essential for your video to make a good first impression. Your videos should be designed to educate, excite, and inspire users to act and download your App instantly. To keep the viewer engaged, it's recommended that your video includes a combination of communication elements: voiceover, featured text, background music, while highlighting your key benefits.

Step #5: Captivating Screenshots

App screenshots take up over 65% of the App Store preview and are the most important visual content that a user will look at. What do Billion Dollar app screenshots from Uber, Airbnb, and Snapchat all have in common? Each screenshot has a purpose and leaves an impact on the viewer. Impact is the impression your promotion makes on its intended target. Your screenshots should be compelling, engaging, and persuasive.

Think of the screenshots you present as the storefront of your business. If you were walking down Main Street and saw a store with ugly and confusing products displayed in the window, would you go inside? Probably not! Yet that's exactly what most beginners have on the App Store. Most simply display boring and confusing screenshots taken directly from the App. This can confuse the viewer. They have no idea what benefits you offer by simply viewing your Apps interface. Remember when it comes to marketing if you confuse, you lose. Don't confuse your potential users.

Effective screenshots are designed to captivate your users' attention and inspire them to action. You must treat your screenshots as if they were your primary marketing assets. Post your screenshots in a logical order that show common user flows. The first screenshot is the most important, so it better give the user a clear idea of the purpose of your

App and why it is better than others on the market. Each screenshot should highlight an important benefit and include at least one line of text to describe it.

Step #6: Compelling Description

When looking at the most successful Apps, you'll find they all follow a specific formula only a select few know about. The proven sequential formula is called AIDA. It stands for **Attention, Interest, Desire, and Action**. This is a formula all great copywriters understand.

1. First, captivate their **ATTENTION**. 98% of users won't read past the first 200 characters. You'd better set the tone with authority.

2. Second, get them **INTERESTED**. Explain why they want YOUR solution.

3. Third, make them **DESIRE** what you offer by articulating the benefits they will receive (not the features).

4. Fourth, inspire them to **ACT** and download the App instantly. Explicitly tell them: download this App now! This is something simple so many Apps on the market miss. It's important to lead the prospect by the hand and inspire them to take direct action now. Otherwise, they'll just continue to browse for other solutions.

Although it's reported only 2% of users will read the full description, it's still important to include the key benefits of your App at the beginning. Unless the user decides to click on the "more" button, they won't see the rest of it. Therefore, your first few sentences must be compelling and include enticing keywords to capture the user's attention quickly.

Step #7: Make It Famous

With hundreds of thousands of competing Apps on the market, what is the quickest and easiest way for you to cut through the noise and clutter to differentiate yourself and establish yourself as a market leader? The answer is by securing high-profile press and media attention around your App launch. When working with the billion-dollar publisher Cheetah Mobile on their Android utility App Security Master, we executed a PR campaign to get the App worldwide recognition on high-profile outlets with millions of visitors. The app was recognized and promoted on The Huffington Post, The Next Web, Entrepreneur, and many others.

By strategically securing high profile media attention on these outlets, it provided a perfect storm of excitement that made the App trend across the web. Security Master now has more than 550,000,000 downloads.

The key is having multiple high-profile outlets with millions of visitors promoting your App at the same time upon launch and recognizing it as the new market leader in your category. When you get everyone promoting your App upon launch or update (preferably within the first 2 weeks), you start trending. As a result, this can make you an instant App celebrity. Not only do you get to secure market validation and brand exposure, but you also get worldwide promotion to millions of visitors to download your App.

Step #8: Make It International/Localized

The magic of launching an App in the App Store or Google Play Store is that you have the potential to reach a worldwide audience. By properly localizing your App, downloads can increase as much as (or even more than) 200%.

If you plan on releasing an App outside of your home country, localize the title, description, and keywords to match that country.

This gives you the opportunity to use extra titles, descriptions, and key-words which ultimately result in higher visibility. The App Stores are in 150 different countries and 40 different languages. Localization is considered one of the easiest ways to increase your App's visibility and downloads. The top five languages experts recommend you target to reach the largest markets are: Chinese, Japanese, German, Korean, and Spanish.

You might be surprised to discover that another country may love your App more than the one it's currently published in. Auto translating /or using Google translating for keywords and descriptions is NOT advised. It can lead to awkward, poor or meaningless keywords, which won't benefit your App at all. Where possible, have native speakers / professional translators help you translate your App Store materials.

Step #9: Attract User Reviews

A major factor that contributes to your ranking and visibility on the App Store and Google Play is the quality and quantity of user reviews. Both App & Google have a process to regularly crawl through your reviews to see what others are saying about your app. Users are also more likely to download Apps with higher ratings. In fact, many of them form a first impression after reading a few reviews. Sending timely push notifications within your App can help you gain more user reviews.

Additionally, obtaining and encouraging user reviews is the perfect way for you to gain feedback on your App and find out which features users love, which they would like to see improved, and which they absolutely despise. You can analyze your ratings to discover what users are thinking.

Step #10: Make It Social

Did you know that 19% of Apps are discovered on social networking platforms? Maintaining active social media pages is crucial for gaining new users and retaining current ones. Social media is an essential part of stimulating conversations about your App. If you've put time and effort into social media and you haven't seen results, then it is time to rethink your game plan!

If you feel fans are not seeing your posts, you may be posting the wrong messages or posting at the wrong times. Facebook and Twitter have optimal times for posting. Facebook's reported optimal times are Monday – Thursday from 11 am – 5 pm EST. Twitter's reported optimal times are Monday – Thursday from 9 am – 3 pm EST. Posting targeted content at certain times will result in a higher rate of user engagement and therefore driving more downloads. Additionally, we have found using Caps Case Typing for the first letter of words draws 52% more re-shares.

App Store Optimization Takes Time and Constant Attention

While ASO has proven to be a critical tool in driving consistent organic downloads, it's not something that happens overnight. The App Store Optimization process takes time and must constantly be improved. It is recommended to analyze and improve your keywords, title, screenshots, videos, and description every few months.

Method #2: Paid Traffic

Paid Traffic is something you can directly control and scale quickly but it comes at a substantial cost. With Paid Traffic, if the stars align and everything goes right, you can quickly go from 0 to 1,000,000 downloads. On the other hand, you can also go broke paying for the wrong advertisement or not having a profitable monetization structure in place.

This type of acquisition method includes buying Search ads, Facebook ads, Twitter ads, YouTube ads, AdWords, and any other cost per install/download method. For this to work you need to have a strong monetization in place (Lifetime Value) to ensure you make more than you spend.

Billion dollar Apps like Clash of Clans, Candy Crush, and Angry Birds spend millions each month on Paid Traffic. As serial entrepreneur Dan Kennedy once said, "Ultimately, the business that can spend the most to acquire a customer wins." This might sound counterintuitive, but it's essential in a world where advertising on Facebook and other channels is getting more expensive. You need to be able to compete against others in your App category. If you can pay more than your competitor to acquire new users and STILL be profitable, you will become the dominate force in your market. When it comes to undergoing Paid Traffic, it's all about sending the right message to the right audience at the right time.

To compare paid traffic to fishing, the bait, the line, and the fishing reel you use is dependent on what you're fishing for. Your potential App users are the hungry fish, your ads are the lures, and every visit is a nibble. But different fish go for different types of lures. Bass go for one lure while trout for another. When I'm fishing for bass, I don't put a trout lure on the line. In the App business, you can't afford to go in blind and just hope for the best.

Whoever Spends the Most to Acquire Users Wins

What has been taught in Universities for generations is the same method traditional businesses use to drive traffic. They set a percentage of their overall budget towards marketing. Typically, that amount is anywhere between 10% and 20%. So, if you have a $100,000 investment in your App, you would allocate $10,000-$20,000 towards marketing. This is how most people think and it's the wrong approach.

Most people put a 10%-20% budget towards this marketing effort because they don't have a predictable outcome. Much like a casino slot machine, they hope to hit a jackpot and have the App go viral. They try different outlets like Facebook ads, Twitter, and AdWords. Instead of a casino slot machine, I recommend looking at paid traffic marketing methods like a vending machine that clearly outlines the price for each outcome. That way you know how much you can spend to get a new user.

Let's say that your App has a lifetime value of $10 from one user. This means over the course of the life of a user engaging your App, you would make $10 in sales. Now let's say it would cost you $5 to acquire that user running Facebook ads. How much of your overall budget would you spend to acquire users? 10%? 20%? 100%? If you can make $10 in sales for each new user and only spend $5 to acquire them, then you would want to spend as much of your budget as possible to get as many users as you can for only $5. This is how Uber, Square, Candy Crush, and the other successful Apps on the market operate regarding paid traffic.

Successful developers narrow their focus and fully understand what it costs to acquire a user through each channel. With the analogy of a vending machine, you should have different options based on different pricing. You could look at it and say, "I could pick the Facebook ads option that's going to cost $5 per download or I could select the Twitter ads option and it may cost me only $4 per download."

Paid advertisements require analysis, discipline and a little courage. If your budget is modest, be very cautious. If your budget is robust, hire a professional to help. Most simply throw money into the wind not knowing any type of predictable result. Instead of using a vending machine, they are simply putting money into the casino's slot machine and hope they get lucky.

- Key Points -

➢ "If you believe in the product or service that you are selling, then you have a moral obligation to do everything in your power to get your product or service in the face of your potential customers." - Jay Abraham

➢ Enter the conversation that exists in your prospect's mind.

➢ People buy out of emotion and justify with logic.

➢ Simple tweaks to your messaging can make the difference between your App succeeding and failing.

➢ It's your messaging that defines the emotional connection users will have with your App.

- Action Steps -

➤ Use the 10 –step "Skyrocket Method" to launch your app success-fully.

➤ How do you want users to feel when they think about your App?

➤ Who is your target market and what do they want?

➤ What keywords are you going to target for users to discover your App?

➤ What message do you want to get across to your potential users?

➤ How do you want users to feel when they first interact with your App?

What's Next?

Ever wonder how billion dollar App creators like Evan Spiegel (Snap-chat), Jack Dorsey (Square), and Brian Chesky (Airbnb) can get so much done and obtain extraordinary results? The key to success is to grow an organization that can build and run itself without you. No matter how smart you are, you need a team that is smarter than you. In the following chapter, we'll uncover how to create a million dollar team.

CHAPTER 7

PILLAR 4: TEAM

lthough we typically look up to the Founder and CEO of a business, there would be no Snapchat without Bobby Murphy. There would be no Uber without Garrett Camp. There would be no Apple without Steve Wozniak. And there would be no Microsoft without Paul Allen. The truth is you can only be as successful as the people with whom you surround yourself. The key is to surround yourself with people that will support you, challenge you and are aligned with what you want to achieve. This is vital to your success.

As author Simon Sinek proclaims, "You can't do it alone. So, don't pretend you can. Life changes for the better when we realize we don't have to know everything. We don't have to pretend we do. This is the reason for teams. It's not simply about capacity; it's about diversity of ideas and strengths. As individuals, we are ok. Together we are formidable. When we work together, we can accomplish anything."

The reality is you're not going to wake up tomorrow and suddenly have everything figured out. Successful people put in the time and money to further advance themselves and their business. They connect with the brightest minds to make it happen. No matter how smart you are, you need a team that is collectively smarter than you. The key to success is to grow an organization that can build and run itself without you.

A Million Dollar App Begins with A Million Dollar Team

Billionaire entrepreneur, Richard Branson built eight different billion-dollar businesses across eight different industries. You would think he knows a little bit about the secrets to success, right?

Well, when asked what was the most fundamental truth that allowed him to build such successful companies? He responded, "It's all about hiring people smarter than you, getting them to join your vision and giving them the right work. Then get out of the way and trust them. You must get out of their way, for you to be able to focus on the bigger vision."

I believe the bigger the dream, the more important the team. Rarely do great businesses or startup ideas go from idea to execution on the shoulders of a single person. That doesn't have as much to do with the 'two heads are better than one' collaboration mentality as it does with the overall combination of resources, knowledge, and connections that enable them to succeed. Founding members tend to get so involved in their own business and operations that they become unable to take a step back and focus on the greater vision.

The following Apps are great stories of how founders and co-founders went from individuals to a single unified unit. They formed bulletproof teams and strived together to meet a common goal.

Real Team Examples:

Airbnb

Nathan Blecharczyk moved to San Francisco in early 2007. He found an apartment and a roommate through Craigslist. That's how he met Joe

Gebbia. Gebbia was a designer and Blecharczyk was an engineer at another startup. Blecharczyk later moved out, and Brian Chesky, who knew Gebbia from the Rhode Island School of Design, moved in. That's how three co-founders came together to solve a problem that what would turn into a $30 billion dollar App business.

Flipboard

As chance would have it, the co-founders of the billion-dollar news aggregation App Flipboard, met on a blind date. Mike McCue and Evan Doll met together at a coffee shop, not yet knowing what they were going to build together in the future.

Obviously, neither did their friends when they set them up; they didn't know McCue and Doll would go about creating an App that was going to revolutionize the way people read the news. With an overload of information available all over the internet, Flipboard was designed to be the App that brings it all together in a clean, easy-to-read format.

Flipboard launched in 2010 exclusively for Apple's iPad, but soon became available on other devices as well. The App was an instant success, praised by industry professionals and users alike. Today, Flipboard is worth around $1 billion. It's currently one of the largest and best-known news aggregator Apps in the world.

Square

Square, an App that made it possible for everyone with a smartphone to receive credit card payments, was founded by three people. Often whenever people talk about Square, the name of Jack Dorsey comes up – the founder of both Square and Twitter – but a lesser known fact is that Square Inc. was founded by three people: Jack Dorsey, Tristan O'Tierney and Jim McKelvey.

Dorsey understood that he couldn't build the prototype on his own and brought on O'Tierney and McKelvey as the iOS developers. An outline of what was soon to become Square started to take shape. The trio, great friends and business partners, went on to develop one of the most innovative and successful Apps of the early 21st century.

Snapchat

Evan Spiegel and Bobby Murphy, the CEO and CTO of Snapchat respectively, met when they were both undergraduate students at Stanford University. At that time, Spiegel studied design and Murphy pursued a degree in computer science.

The two of them went on to become the force behind the App that revolutionized the way today's younger generations communicate. Snapchat's story is in many ways like that of Facebook – three people started developing it, but not all ended up reaping the full benefits. The most interesting thing about the genesis of Snapchat was that Spiegel and Murphy had a third partner back in the earliest days of the App, when it was still called Picaboo. His name was Reggie Brown, another Stanford University student.

As often happens with startups, early business partnerships are volatile and friendships are fragile. Sometimes people don't see eye to eye, either professionally or personally and go their separate ways. In the end, Snapchat's Reggie Brown was compensated for his role in the app's early development. Under the skillful guidance of Spiegel and Murphy, Snapchat became one of the most recognizable and popular communication Apps on the planet.

You Can't 10X Your Business with A 1X Team

Regardless of how driven you are, if you decide to take on building a successful App by yourself, you will be at a major disadvantage. A dataset analysis conducted by Startup Genome including 100,000 existing startups reveals that it takes 3.6 times longer for solo founders to reach the startup scale stage as compared to businesses launched by a founding team of at least two members.

If you want your product or service to grow successfully, statistics shows you need to partner up. A recent analysis of U.S. based private and public market startups with an overall worth more than $1 billion dollars, published by Tech Crunch, showed startups that have an average of 3 founders with a complementary set of skills last significantly longer than teams of 1 or 2. In a sense, Steve Jobs was a textbook example. He was quirky and, as many say, difficult to work with. Yet, even he could not take the world by storm by himself. He needed Steve Wozniak.

Peter Thiel, the founder of PayPal and Palantir (both billion dollar successes), attests the eccentricity of PayPal's founders was a major factor for its accomplishments. Thiel believes the key to PayPal's success was the extreme set of traits jointly displayed by its co-founding team.

I found that in the early stages of the App, the CEO tries to do everything. The truth is you don't need to do and learn everything (nor should you). It is impossible to know and do everything in business. Instead discover and focus your time on your own unique abilities and hire others that can perform the needed tasks better than you. What are you best at and the most passionate about? What is your unique ability? What is your super power? Are you the Hustler, Product Manager or Growth Hacker?

It is important to be competent in various sectors of the business, but you're not going to be able to solve and do everything. Do not worry about incremental growth but focus on where you can truly excel. I encourage you to forget about improving your weaknesses. Instead double down on what you're great at. Have tunnel vision and focus on your unique abilities.

How to Build a Million Dollar Team

Silicon Valley serial-entrepreneur Steve Blank, author of 'The Startups Owner Manual,' recognized startups are chaotic by nature and that squeezing the chaos into a marketable product needs to be done by a founding team with an adequate set of skills. It's important to be clear on the roles and responsibility of the business leaders.

I am often asked, "How big should my team be?" The optimal size of your team will vary depending on many different factors, including the type of App (social network, business, game, fitness, transportation, etc.) and how many active users you have. For example, before being acquired by Facebook, Instagram had only 13 employees. On the other hand, Uber currently has over 6,700 employees, excluding the drivers.

Your team members must embrace great technological skills, including those who have a knack for top-notch UX design, long-term vision and product sense. The technology infrastructure must be supported by someone who knows how to leverage the right business model, get to the proper market and use the right messaging.

A single person can have one or two of these basic sets of skills. This is why tech entrepreneurs share the opinion that prosperous startups need to be founded by two or three people. For an effective and productive team DNA, I believe each early stage startup member usually adopts one or two of the three key roles - a Hustler, a Product Manager, and a Hacker.

Ideal Team DNA

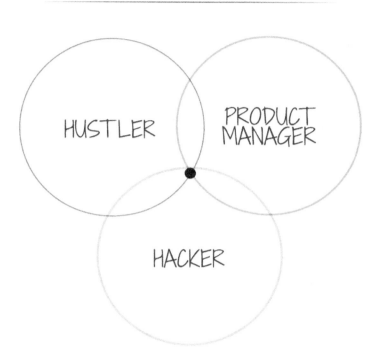

Hustlers - Build Relationships

The Hustler is ultimately the visionary. The visionary primarily focuses on the "What" and the "Why" of the business. What is the plan? What is the next step? What is the end goal? Why are we doing it?

The Hustler is a communicator that never loses sight of the big picture. Even the brightest vision packed into the perfect product needs a skilled person who can effectively enroll customers, find partners and attract investors into the App. The Hustler is the face of the company and CEO.

Although they may not all admit it, Steve Jobs, Jack Dorsey, and Mark Zuckerberg are all Hustlers.

The role of the hustler is to literally interpret a world that others don't even know exists yet and bring it into fruition. The Hustler on your team will take on what has been carefully crafted as an idea in private and bring it into the public light by enrolling other team members, speaking at conferences, negotiating deals and building the right messaging around the App.

Hustlers not only can articulate their vision clearly, but can get others equally passionate as well. They are also the masters of creating business relationships where people, products and business operations flow to profits with ease. Building a million dollar App business requires building better relationships with your employees, advisers, mentors, investors and partners. These relationships build social capital and can be one of the strongest resources in your arsenal. It will help build trust, understanding and loyalty that allow the business to thrive even in uncertain times.

One of the best skills you can acquire is to understand how to better communicate with others to maximize efficiency and results. To fully maximize the unique traits of a visionary, they must stay focused on high-level growth and operations. The problem many visionaries face though is a lack of focus (most have Attention Deficit Disorder) and an inability to let go and delegate key roles and responsibilities.

Product Managers – Execute

A Product Manager is ultimately the integrator. This person has the gift of translating the vision into execution and completion. Project Managers focus on the "How" and the "Who." How are we going to do this? Who will execute and be responsible for each task?

Many startup CEO's get so carried away with their vision and with business managing funding, recruiting and operations, they forget about product practicality. As execution experts, Product Managers know how to discern the thin line between a product mirage and a product that lives with market trends.

Steve Jobs' main strength was his visionary capacity, but he would have undeniably been less successful if he didn't have an army of highly skilled Product Managers (developers) who could execute his vision. They are the unsung heroes. Your Product Manager can make the impossible possible. They transform the vision into reality.

Growth Hackers - Get Downloads

Growth Hackers are ultimately the marketing growth engineers. They are problem solvers and typically in charge of growth marketing and growth hacking to reach critical mass. Growth hackers strategically focus on the "Where" in a measurable and scientific way. Where can we get quality downloads at an affordable cost? Where are our most engaged users coming from? With growth hacking, the initiatives are typically driven by ROI. They focus on what is testable, measurable, and scalable.

They find diverse solutions to a problem that excites them and gets them going until they reach an ideal result. A Growth Hacker observes the problem in a unique and special way, through the lens of potential solutions. They are ultimately aimed at strategically meeting the business goals by acquiring more downloads, users, and sales.

What Are Your Unique Abilities?

What is it that makes you unique? Are you the Hustler? Are you the Growth Hacker? Or are you the Product Manager? Understand what your unique ability is and find others that can complement yours.

It's important to find others who see the world through a different lens than you do, have complementary skills, and the ability to work through a disagreement. As 'Fast Company' author Dan Lambert states "Knowing how you will handle a bumpy road is something you should assess early, honestly, and head-on. Startup life isn't always rainbows and butterflies, though, and you should be prepared for difference of opinions and disagreements."

When growing your team, it's important to help others learn how to be their best every day and condition them with the right mindset. To ensure everyone is fully aligned with the right objectives at hand, in his book 'Scaling Up,' author Verne Harnish recommends doing a daily huddle with everyone on your team for 10 minutes. During this daily meeting, have each member answer the following questions:

- What initiatives have been working for you?

- What's your number one priority for today?

- Give a quick update on your goals and key performance metrics.

- Where are you stuck?

What Is Your Time Worth?

The three wealthiest people in the world – Warren Buffett, Jeff Bezos and Bill Gates – each has 1,440 minutes in a day to earn money. So do you. The most educated man in the world has 168 hours in a week to learn. So do you. The greatest athlete in the world has 365 days in a year to train. So do you.

Those that make most of their time, win. Billion dollar app creators know how to control their time and not let time control them. How? By scheduling, prioritizing, and most importantly leveraging your most productive time to do asset-producing tasks. Become a master for the clock. Rich people buy time while the poor waste time.

Do you dominate your 525,600 minutes each year or does time dominate you? For you to achieve great results you must focus on your time and control it. We all have the same 24-hours in a day. You can choose to spend your time doing $10/hour tasks or $10,000/hour tasks to further your App business. I can guarantee you won't be able to build and market a million dollar App focusing on $10/hour tasks. As John Maxwell says "Nothing separates successful people from unsuccessful people more than how they use their time."

Did you know the highest paid brain surgeons only perform 3 tasks? When they go into surgery everything is already prepped for them. All they do is what they have mastered for years, and perform 3 precise brain surgical tasks. When they're done, they don't even sew up the patient. Why? Because they understand what their time is worth.

You don't see Even Spiegel spending days on end at the computer fixing a technical issue with Snapchat, do you? You don't' see Travis Kalanick driving Uber passengers, do you? None of the Founders of the top Apps code, design, or operate the App anymore. Why? Not necessarily because they do not want to, but simply because it's not the best use of their time. They could make themselves crazy spending hundreds of hours refining the code, design and marketing. Instead they hire experts to do it for them and achieve greater results in the process. They focus on their unique abilities and tasks that only they can do and delegate everything else to others that perform them even better.

We all have weapons of mass distraction, and if you let it, your weapon of mass distraction will sink your ships and destroy your productivity. A main driver to failure of any app business is the lack of focusing the resources of money, time, and energy on the wrong initiatives. It's focusing on the right actions over time that will make your app a success. It's no surprise that the most successful people focus and evoke maximum amount of time to be productive on their top priority.

I have found that the secret method the most successful app creators perform is a system called 'Time Blocking'. They block time in their calendar to work on the one thing that will give them the greatest results. 'Time Blocking' is a results oriented way to ensure what has to get done actually gets done. By blocking out time it automatically harnesses your energy and allows you focus on your most important work.

Power of Delegation & Outsourcing

The more of your business you can systematize, automate or delegate gives you time and energy to focus on your role as business owner. The result is greater innovation and creativity. Business owners should focus on high level initiatives like building traffic, downloads and sales.

What areas of your work can you systematize, automate, or delegate? A fundamental problem I've found is many creators try and delegate miracles. They delegate items hoping others can magically fix a problem that in most cases the CEO or Founder needs to solve themselves. They will delegate to someone or hire an agency to get 10 million downloads and say "this will solve having a crappy product". You need a certain understanding of the operation before delegating it to another.

Know your strengths, and outsource your weaknesses. If you're just starting out consider how you can outsource some of your tasks to allow you to grow. Outsourcing refers to the way in which you entrust business functions to external vendors. The benefits of outsourcing include cost advantages, increased efficiency, and time-zone advantage. The main problems that can arise with outsourcing, however, can be quality and communication issues.

The Startup Killer

The #1 early startup killer is not a lack of App revenue, technology or inadequate funding. In fact, according to a study reported by Founder-AndFouders.com, 62% of startups fail due to conflict between co-founders. Even before an App has been launched, one of the #1 App startup killers is co-founder conflict.

Co-founders clashing and tearing the business apart, is the fastest way to its demise. I've personally launch dozens of businesses and 50% of them failed due to co-founder conflict. Why do most co-founders feud? Mostly they feud over growth decisions, equity distribution, and finances. If you can get your agreements in writing up front, it will save you significant problems in the future.

As author Jeff Haden from Inc. Magazine shares, "Talent is obviously important, but the ability to work together, to check egos at the door, and to make individual sacrifices when necessary is the only way a team succeeds. With great teams, it's never about you. It's always, always, always about the team. Think about the business teams you've seen fail. Rarely was the failure due to a lack of talent. More often, those teams failed because of personality conflicts, ego clashes, or competing agendas."

Co-Founder Vesting

One of the most common mistakes that startup businesses seem to repeatedly make is that they issue stock to the company's founders without imposing any restrictions on that stock. Everyone involved in the startup of a business assumes everything will go smoothly and that they'll all just get along for the long-term and make millions of dollars. I cannot over-emphasize just how big of a mistake that is.

In most startup businesses, at least one co-founder is likely to drop out eventually. The problem comes when a co-founder leaves with full ownership of their share of the stock. Co-founder vesting is when the shares held by the founder become subject to a contractual right of repurchase, often at a nominal value, if the founder is no longer providing services to the company.

Billionaire investor Andreessen Horowitz wrote an article for Fortune.com titled 'Your Next Business Partner Should Come with a Prenup,' where he stated, "It is well understood that it is in the best interest of the company, its employees, its investors and the remaining co-founders to make sure that if a founder voluntarily quits for some reason, he does not get to retain all of his equity. In fact, most startups nowadays have a three to four-year vesting period for the founders' shares."

It is completely unfair that a co-founder can be allowed to leave a company after just a week or two, yet retain all their stock. That's why it's so important to have a signed, legal agreement in place from the beginning that outlines the co-founder vesting details. A restricted stock purchase agreement addresses vesting schedules. This schedule requires each co-founder to execute it so a business retains the right to repurchase un-vested shares of the company at the initial purchase price. You absolutely must have this in place if you want to avoid future problems.

Find Mentors & Advisors

Do you want to be the best? It's simple. Surround yourself with the best. I have learned the people you decide to surround yourself with will tend to either elevate or lower your standards. They either help you become the lowest version of yourself or the highest. I encourage you to surround yourself with others that raise your standards and challenge you to become the best version of yourself.

The key to reaching extraordinary results is taking massive action and effective execution, which is all about modeling others. If you can find and model the best example of those that succeeded before you, then you can compress the time it took to make it happen. You should be standing on the shoulders of people around you instead of trying to re-invent the wheel. The benefits of mentors and advisors are invaluable to your business startup. The Startup Genome dataset report affirmed that startups with advisors raise 7x more funds and have 3.5x greater growth than the rest.

For every billion dollar App, their advisors were vital for the startup progress to scale and reach critical mass. Having a board of advisors can be critical to your app's prosperity. Experienced advisors can jump in with ready answers to typical challenges including salaries, development, investments, growth and marketing. Having the right advisor will profoundly save you time and money. The role of a startup advisor is less burdened by business rules. It is precisely this informal aspect that can help your team find the right answers when you hit the daily nitty-gritty.

The smartest business decision I ever made was to hire my first business coach. We all need a coach. Lebron James, Michael Phelps, Tom Brady and every professional athlete at the pinnacle of performance always had a coach. Mark Zuckerberg has one. Warren Buffett has one. Steve Jobs had one. You can't succeed without proper coaching, let alone trying to do it all on your own.

So how do you find a coach or advisor? The reality is that we live in a world where everyone is digitally interconnected online. On Facebook or LinkedIn, you are only 3 connections away from someone who has already achieved the success you set out for. This could be someone who has received outside funding for their App, has 10,000,000 downloads or sold their App to Apple. Go find them! They are more willing to help you than you might think. They were once in your shoes.

I am constantly working to build my network with the most inspirational and brilliant minds. I know that's the key to my own success. Find people who are trying to improve themselves the same way you are. Surround yourself with people who inspire you and make you a better person. Only choose people whom you respect and look up to.

- Key Points -

➤ A million dollar App begins with a million dollar team.

➤ The key to success is to grow an organization that can build and run itself without you.

➤ You can only be as successful as the people you surround yourself with.

➤ Successful people put in the time and money to further advance themselves and their business.

➤ What is it that makes you unique? Are you the Hustler? Are you the Growth Hacker? Or are you the Product Manager? Understand what your unique ability is and find others that can complement yours.

➤ Startups that have an average of 3 founders with a complementary set of skills last significantly longer than teams of 1 or 2 founders.

➤ You can't succeed without proper coaching.

➤ Surround yourself with people who inspire you, who make you better, whom you respect and look up to.

➤ You can only be as successful as the people you surround yourself with.

- Action Step -

➤ What are your unique abilities?

➤ What work can you delegate to focus on more important tasks?

➤ What areas can you systematize and automate?

➤ Create a list of online groups, masterminds, and events you can join to further advance yourself.

➤ Create a list of the top successful individuals to reach out and help you on your journey to become your advisor or coach.

What's Next?

How does an app go viral? How can you make your App truly indispensable? In the following chapter I'll uncover how today's smartest Apps like Snapchat, Candy Crush, and Tinder become indispensable and a daily habit for millions of people.

CHAPTER 8

PILLAR 5: VIRALITY, RETENTION, APP ADDICTION

E very App creator ultimately seeks two things: **(1)** They want their App to become a Viral success. **(2)** They need customers to retain, update and use the App several times each day. They want their App to be so addictive that users subconsciously feel they must consistently use it on a daily basis. I call this Virality, Retention and App Addiction.

Virality Is Not Luck, It's Engineered

Virality is a marketing term that refers to the phenomenon of a product or service experiencing exponential growth over a short period of time. Every day I am asked by others, "How can I make my App go viral?"

My answer is always the same. Deliver an exceptional experience people will never be able to forget. If you build something people really want and give them a compelling reason to share it, your customers will grow your App business for you. I know this is something most creators don't like to hear. Most want to learn the secret hacks that work now.

Apps don't go viral by accident. Virality is strategically engineered. How did Pokémon Go reach 500 Million downloads in less than a year? How did Snapchat reach mass adoption in such a short time period? How do you attract, maintain, and multiply this activity in an efficient way?

The answer is to implement what I call Viral Growth Engines. Viral Growth Engines are about leveraging viral mechanics embedded <u>within</u> the App to reach millions of downloads. As Jonah Berger, author of 'Contagious: Why Things Catch On,' explains, "Virality isn't luck. It's not magic. And it's not random. There's a science behind why people talk and share. A recipe. A formula, even."

The framework behind a viral loop is simple and looks like this:

- A user downloads an App and likes it
- He/she is offered a small incentive to share the app
- He/she shares the App with a friend
- Those friends download the app
- The cycle continues

Facebook sends invitations. Dropbox offers free space if a user refers a friend. Instagram offers cross-posting to other social media venues. These incentives cause conversations, which lead to referrals. These referrals get others to try the product, and voila, viral growth occurs.

Viral Growth Engines

The term "Growth Hacker" has become an overused buzzword over the past decade. My favorite definition of a Growth Hacker is by Ryan Holiday in his book, 'Growth Hacker Marketing,' he says, "A growth hacker is someone who has thrown out the playbook of traditional marketing and replaced it with only what is testable, measurable, and scalable. While their marketing brethren chase vague notions like 'branding' and 'mind share', growth hackers relentlessly pursue users and growth — when they do it right, those users beget more users, who beget more users. They are the innovators, operators, and mechanics of their own self-sustaining and self-propagating growth machine that can take a start up from nothing to something."

With growth hacking, the initiatives are driven by ROI (Return on In-vestment). Finding users and getting downloads for your App is no long-er about playing guessing games. Instead, it's about using mathematical formulas. Real growth engines have nothing to do with miracle hacks. Companies such as Uber, Facebook, and Twitter have entire teams ded-icated to growth through strategic engineering and product design. These organizations view themselves as expert Growth Engineers rather than Hackers. In truth, growth is not achieved through a specific hack or a quick trick. App developers who resort to gimmicks typically have not built a quality product.

Viral products generate exponential growth because they leverage each acquired customer and build a self-sustaining user acquisition machine. The key is to give your users a compelling reason to share your App with others such that others repeat this behavior. This is different from tradi-tional marketing funnels, which are designed to reach the masses to convert a small group of end users.

Viral Funnel

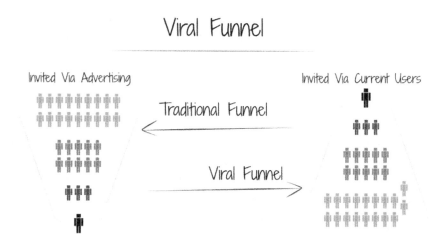

Virality is measurable. Here is an example of Virality by the numbers. Let's say an app started with 100 users and they were each enticed to invite 15 new users. That's 1,500 invitations! Can that happen? You bet it can. That's what incentives are all about. Of course not all of those invitees decide to download but let's say 10% of them do. That's 150 new   users!

For those interested in formulas the viral coefficient (k) is the number of new users generated divided by the number of original users 150/100 = k. In this case k = 1.5. The lesson in all this is your existing user base can explode into viral growth if their experience is good and they are enticed to invite a lot of new users. Meaning for every new users you have, they bring 1.5 more users to the app.

Dropbox's Growth Engine

The founders of Dropbox had an important choice to make early in their business. They could either continue to repeat their initial tactic of using powerful videos to reel in customers, or they could boost their presence with paid advertising. They decided to use paid advertising but quickly learned that it cost them $233 to $388 for each paying subscriber.

That discovery led them to an epiphany of sorts. They chose to do something innovative. Using an idea brought forth by Sean Ellis, Dropbox changed the game by creating one of the most viral referral programs in the world. What makes this even more extraordinary is that the idea was simple. All they did was place a button on the front page of their service that said, "Get Free Space."

This offer gave current users 500MB of free space for each friend they referred and got to sign up to Dropbox. The referral process was incredibly simple to use which allows users to connect to Gmail and easily add friends' emails. As a result, Dropbox went from 100,000 to 4,000,000 users in 15 months, a 40X increase, doubling users every 3 months. According to Dropbox's CEO Drew Houston, Dropbox users have now created 3.3 billion connections by sharing with each other, with now 500 million total signups. The company is currently valued at over $10 billion.

It's amazing how such a simple idea could be so effective. This teaches us two important facts:

1. Breakthroughs do not need to be overly complicated. They are usually simple ideas that get extraordinary results.

2. Referrals are KING! They absolutely rule the marketing world.

Even today, approximately 35% of Dropbox subscribers are referrals. If you want your App to go viral, you MUST include some sort of referral program. Once you start seeing the world through this lens, you will begin spotting opportunities for growth. You can't just release an App and expect people to just share it. They need to be motivated to pass it around with incentives and an easy process to share it.

The "Viral App Blueprint"

As I worked with, interviewed and studied some of the fastest growing Apps whose tactics contributed to this book, I noticed that each had used different sets of strategies that contributed to dramatically increasing downloads and sales over a short period of time.

I have compiled the best strategies and learned that today's successful viral Apps share the following characteristics in what I call the "Viral App Blueprint." This Blueprint breaks down the most successful Viral Growth Engine strategies that top Apps use to drive millions of downloads. Once you have first incorporate the "Skyrocket Method" shared in the previous chapter and reached some initial traction with the app, the next step is to implement the strategies outlined in this Blueprint.

Viral App Blueprint

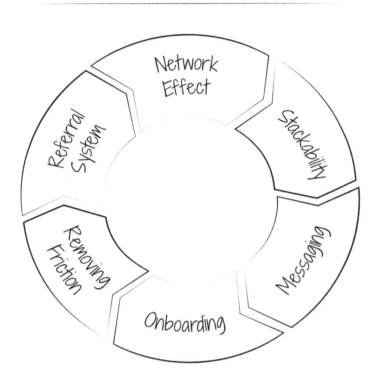

1. Win-Win Referral System

From my experience, the fastest growing Apps that go viral have dou-ble-sided incentives or what I like to call a "Win-Win Strategy." This strategy benefits both the person sharing the App and the recipient. To scale up to a million dollar App, incorporating a win-win referral system is one of the most important growth engine techniques you must mas-ter. It's important to do more than simply rely on standard social media tactics to encourage users to share your App with others.

Many believe simply incorporating social features like Facebook and Twitter integration will make their App go viral. This is far from the truth. Simply adding social sharing within your App or integrating Facebook sign up will NOT make your App go viral.

Earlier, I shared the importance of having a referral strategy. Most fail in this strategy by not having a compelling incentivized offer to share the App. To be a success at this, a <u>Win-Win Strategy</u> needs the following three qualities:

I.   The incentive makes the user look "good" to the people they invite. People, obviously, won't share something that will negatively affect their status with their peers. However if you can elevate their status and make them look good to their peers the referrals will skyrocket.

II. The incentive gives real value to the user when the invited person joins. For example, Uber's "split fare" feature or Groupon's "buy this deal together" offer. Users want to share Uber so they can easily split the fare with them. Users want to share Groupon so they can take advantage of a better deal. In both cases, people are referring non-users to their product while adding value to the App.

III. They give real value to the people that were invited once they sign up. Airbnb provides new users credit towards their first stay while Instacart provides referral recipients $10 off their first order. Uber offers a $25 credit towards your first ride.

From Uber to Groupon, the biggest marketing breakthroughs came from effective hooks, offers and solutions... or a combination of the three. What incentive can you offer for others to share your app? Can you unlock a certain In-App purchase for free in exchange for sharing and downloading the app?

If you can provide your users with an irresistible offer and incentivize them to share your App, whether through unlocking a private level, offering an achievement banner, or providing bonus points/ currency, you will build a growth engine that will grow your App for you. These referral features should be tied to the core experience of your app. Building an extension of these organic interactions into your app will result in the highest conversion rates for new users.

2. User Generated Content / Network Effect

This is established when your users are in charge of creating content and value within the App. For example, Facebook, YouTube, Snapchat, and Twitter are based on user generated content and engagement. The more people who join, the more others have an incentive to join and the greater the value. Is there any aspect of your App you can either allow or expand user generated content? How can you build or expand your community so that the larger the network the more others will want to be a part of it?

3. Stackability

This is when a viral network is integrated with another, each fostering the others' growth. It was through a combination of savvy marketing and smart engineering that let Airbnb's early team to figure out how to automatically cross-post to Craigslist for available bookings, even though Craigslist offered no APIs. The result? The site became a major driver of traffic, links, and new users for Airbnb early on. One of the largest attributors to YouTube's early success was its seamless integration with MySpace. Therefore, they leveraged the MySpace community to get more YouTube members for free. Is there an existing large network that your App can integrate with that will simultaneously enhance the experience for your users and allow you to leverage the traffic of another network?

4. Master Your Messaging

The better the messaging, the more users will be able to understand, use, and share the App. The messaging within your App defines your product. When thinking about your product, constantly calibrate your messaging. In the process, you might come up with an amazing phrase that is simpler for your customers to <u>understand</u> and <u>share</u> with others. When you can explain your App concisely, you are on your way to being significantly more user friendly.

Think about the phrase "Share Photos" versus "Store Photos." On the surface, they look the same, but each phrase leads you to download something completely different. The term "Share Photos" can relate to Facebook or Instagram, while the term "Store Photos" can relate to Apps such as Dropbox.

In a blog post in 2011 Uber's co-founder Travis Kalanick stated, "95% of all our riders have heard about Uber from other Uber riders. Our virality is almost unprecedented. For every 7 rides we do, our users' big mouths generate a new rider. Imagine if Twitter got a new user every 7 tweets? Wait, maybe they do..."

If someone were to share your App with a friend and describe it in just 2-3 words, what would you want them to say?

5. Optimize Your Onboarding Experience

Onboarding is the first process users go through after downloading and opening the App. It's the process of new user adoption. By improving your onboard experience, you drastically improve the number of engaged users, shares, and revenue. During this period, do not offer boring introduction screens or waste time with more marketing language. All of the top Apps on the market have been designed to drive their users to act and get value from the app as quickly as possible. Enhancing the onboarding experience can result in a 30% to 50% increase in conversions from 'install' to 'user activation.'

The users who have installed your App have already expressed an interest in using it. Now is the time to "WOW" them. According to the App analytics agency Localytics, 75% of users will stop using an App after 90 days. Your App can't go viral if people don't use it, right?

Consider how you can teach users the necessary skills to be successful. I recommend replacing traditional welcome screens with a compelling video or a guided walkthrough that allows users to learn about your App by using it. When people learn as they go, they will understand the context of an action and ultimately take those actions in real time.

You can also move users forward by providing positive reinforcement. Studies have shown that adding a progress bar can increase conversions up to 40%. People feel compelled to finish something when they know they are almost done. Also, consider including green check marks that appear inside your account creation fields and animations between screens to thank users for taking high friction actions.

6. Remove Friction

Friction occurs when too many irrelevant options cause confusion within an App, resulting in App abandonment. If you confuse, you lose. A common design trend among the most successful Apps is simplicity. How easy is it to have users get to their desired outcome quickly? Whether it's advancing to the next level of a game, ordering a taxi, or booking a plane ticket, it's critical to remove friction to get users to their desired outcome as quickly as possible. With each major App update, Uber strategically removes friction in both design and functionality to make it easier to order a car.

Creators often over-complicate their App and jam it with too many features. When this happens, users are less likely to act. Understand where your App's core value "WOW" factor is, then remove excess friction to achieve it. Ask yourself how you can easily move users forward in an intuitive and painless manner.

Great design eliminates the friction and the effort that it takes to do a specific behavior. Innovation is about reducing the steps between the user's need and the user's reward. Design the App so the user can get to their desired result as easily as possible.

Retention = Growth

Most App creators focus so much on getting new users they forget all about their existing ones. It's much easier to turn potential users into active, paying users than to go out and find brand new prospects. What the top Apps understand, that many beginner Apps do not, is that retention = growth. As an App creator and marketer, your job is to drive potential users to your App AND create lifelong loyal fans. It should be no surprise that dedicated and happy users are the most loyal and also the best marketing tools you can have.

According to Market Metrics, the probability of selling to an existing customer is 60% to 70%. The probability of selling to a new prospect is just 5% to 20%. It's also far easier to keep a loyal user, than it is to acquire a new one. In his book 'The Lean Startup', Eric Ries writes, "The focus needs to be on improving customer retention. Forgo the conventional wisdom that says if a company lacks growth, it should invest more in sales and marketing. It should instead invest in refining and improving the service itself until users are so happy they can't stop using the service (and their friends come along with them)." Bain & Company released a report stating a 5% boost in customer retention can increase profits in a company by 30%!

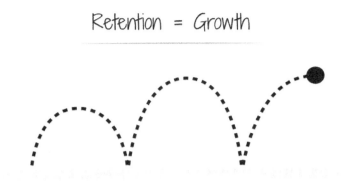

Simply put, the more that a user uses an App, the more they are willing to pay for it, and share it with others. When you increase the frequenting of usage, you not only increase your sales (LTV) but also your user growth as you begin to supercharge in App sharing. This provides more opportunities to encourage others to invite their friends and share their engagement on social channels.

Twitter

In its early days, Twitter had a major issue with its retention. People would create an account but never end up using the service or coming back again. As a result, they did what all of the top entrepreneurs do when they have a problem. They poured over their user statistics to pinpoint the exact problem. What they discovered was that when a user manually followed at least five people on their first day, they were more likely to stay than users who did not follow anyone.

This new information was vital because it allowed growth engineer Josh Elman to navigate Twitter in a way that addressed that metric. His team would add a user flow that encouraged users to follow at least five people upon their initial login. This one simple addition to the onboarding process began to dramatically reduce the churn rate so they took it a step further by adding a feature that "recommends" people for you to follow.

Those two changes were quite simple, yet they made a profound impact on the success of Twitter in its early days. It was so successful that it would become a standard for all social media networks. For example, Facebook has its "people you might know" in the sidebar.

Stealing Time from Other Apps

Most people use up to 7 Apps every day. The ultimate goal for any app creator is to be a member of this club. All Apps on the market ultimately compete for the same limited mindshare. This arms race of users attention is led by Facebook, Google, Snapchat and WhatsApp. How can you stealing away users from the competition? If someone is bored or lonely, how can you get them to use your App instead of browsing Facebook? To accomplish this, you need to change your users' daily routines.

The "Toothbrush Test"

How often must someone use your App for it to be a winner? Eric Schmidt, Chairman of Google outlines in his book 'How Google Works' says everything they build at Google has to pass the "Toothbrush Test." This means people MUST use an App at least twice a day. If users don't, it won't generate the mindshare needed to drive significant revenue. The secret to crafting an addicting App is encouraging habitual behavior. It must become a part of daily life. Something one automatically does every day.

Let's look at Netflix as an example. Netflix has become an indispensable App and is used daily by millions worldwide. What features drive this need? One of the main features in Netflix is the ability to build a personal playlist called 'My List'. 'My List' invests users in the platform and builds on its value. Additionally the Trigger that automatically starts the next episode after watching drives users to continually engage.

In its quarterly letter to investors, Netflix stated its members streamed 42.5 billion hours' worth of programming in 2015. Each individual subscriber spent 568 hours watching Netflix in 2015. That's 1 hour and 33 minutes per day of streaming. I'd say this passes the "Toothbrush Test!"

Make Your App an Everyday Habit

How can you make your App truly indispensable? Apps that become first to our mind win. Habit-forming Apps link their services to the daily routines and emotions of their users.

A habit is an automatic, often subconscious behavior. Our brain creates habits to save energy. Whenever we perform a habitual behavior, our neural activity is lower, ruling out other parts of our brain (such as willpower) to perform a routine. For some people, checking Facebook or Snapchat is as normal as brushing their teeth. It's a habit. It's a routine.

Bumble is a new, popular competing dating App to Tinder. So why haven't more Tinder users switched to Bumble? If a user is familiar with Tinder's features, switching to Bumble requires effort. Habit-forming Apps keep users loyal. They no longer need to think about whether to use Tinder when they feel lonely or lack of connection. They use it without thinking, because it's a habit.

If you want to build your App so that it becomes a habit-forming product, you must be able to identify what your users' internal habits are. What's the psychological need that drives them to use your app? If you were to enter the conversation in your user's mind, what internal emotional state do they need to be in to value your app? What's the thing that occurs frequently that will drive a user to use your App once or twice a day?

How do you create an App where whenever someone is lonely, they use your dating App instead of others? Whenever someone is hungry, they use your food delivery App instead of others? Whenever someone is bored, they use your game instead of using others? In his book 'Hooked,' author Nir Eyal outlined the systematic framework for how products and services become a part of daily life. He describes how products become a habitual behavior and indispensable.

As Eyal says, "Hooks connect the user's problem with a company's solution frequently enough to form a habit. An addicting App contains a trigger, routine action, a reward and investment." I adapted Eyal's "Hooked Method" to the App ecosystem. The following is a breakdown of the App Addition Framework that, when combined and incorporated correctly, can make practically any App become indispensable to its users.

In the following blueprint I'll uncover how today's smartest Apps like Snapchat, Candy Crush, and Tinder become indispensable and a daily habit for millions of people. The following 'Hooked Method' will give you the power to influence the behaviors of everyday lives of billions of users.

App Addiction Method

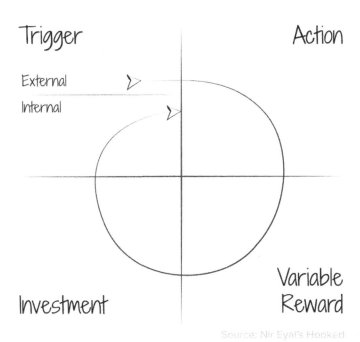

Trigger

Action

External

Internal

Investment

Variable
Reward

Source: Nir Eyal's Hooked

The App "Addiction Method"

Step #1: Trigger

A trigger stimulates users to act and use the App. It's the core reason why people want to use it in the first place. There is no need to use your App without some sort of trigger. There are two types of Triggers: External and Internal.

Internal Trigger – Prompts us to act based on our previous emotional or preexisting habits. These triggers were promoted by our internal feelings to drive us to a certain App, based on our emotional state. An internal trigger could be hunger or boredom. For example, if we feel lonely we go on Facebook, Tinder or YouTube. Hunger triggers us to order food from Grubhub or Seamless.

Without the need of connection or FOMO (Fear of Missing Out), users wouldn't use Snapchat. According to Snap Inc.'s initial public offering prospectus, 158 million people are using Snapchat every single day. On average, users open the App 18 times a day. This is the type of engagement you want to create for your App.

External Trigger – Prompts us to act based on an external feature. External triggers are typically generated through an advertisement, button, design, or message. They are external features that tell us to do something such as push the play button, push the buy button, share, or when a push notification appears. Facebook sends triggers every time someone messages or tags you. When a user gets a notification, intrigue is created. A dating App called The League sends out catchy push notification at specific times every day to remind users that new matches are available.

How to Implement: What external triggers can you use to remind users to reengage with the app? Identify the pain or pleasure point your users encounter at an emotional level, rather than a product feature. What emotional state will they be in when using the app? What actions can you use to entice the user further and remind them to use your app? Give them a message that responds to these elements. To create a new routine, a user must get used to going from trigger to action quickly.

Step #2: Action

Action is what users do to start using a product. Action is simply the initiation someone takes in anticipation of a reward. Whether users act or not depends on their current motivation. The best product designers aim to simplify this process so it becomes as easy as possible to act. Through design, you can improve a user's ability to act by making the intended task easier to complete for them. Examples consist of:

➢ Hitting the play button to see a video instantly.

➢ Scrolling down the newsfeed to view a friend's post.

➢ Swiping right and instantly matching with someone on Tinder.

In many cases one action is a trigger for another. Going back to the Snapchat example, the action occurs as every new message sent initiates a response to reply. The recipient can take the next action by easily tapping the original message to reply. Snapchat's built-in timer encourages a back and forth replay that entices users to keep coming back throughout the day.

For Uber, the users' action is ordering a ride within the App. Uber has reported it initiates more than 1 million rides per day. That is a lot of actions! The easier it is for the user to take action and get to their desired outcome, the more valuable your App will be.

How to Implement: Make it as easy as possible for users to take steps forward and consistently obtain value from your App. Show them how to efficiently move forward and be delighted in the process.

Step #3: Variable Reward

The variable reward is the result of the user taking action. If one expects a reward from an action, the brain experiences a dopamine high. Dopamine is the hormone responsible for cravings. Once the brain learns there is a reward for taking an action, the trigger stimulates stronger motivation. The trick is variability, which multiplies this process and stimulates a gambling-like behavior. The key is to create a craving and ongoing desire.

Sometimes you get your desired outcome and sometimes you don't. That's why gambling is so addictive. Sometimes you win and sometimes you lose. If you lost every single time, you probably wouldn't return. What makes Pokémon Go and Tinder so addicting is the unexpected result and variable reward. It's the uncertainty that keeps users engaged.

Pokémon Go can surprise users by hiding different Pokémon in unique locations. If you matched with someone every single time you swiped right on Tinder, it would become too easy. The element of surprise would be lost. At some point, you would use the App less frequently. But if you visit multiple times a day, you are seeking out the variable reward of matching with someone you are interested in. Tinder reported to the New York Times in 2015 that users log in 11 times a day on average, spending more than 60 minutes each day.

Surfing Facebook, checking Instagram, and shopping on Amazon become mindless habits repeated constantly, without boredom, because they give a variable reward. There is uncertainty and anticipation of what you might find. There can be a picture of your friend in Hawaii or you could find your latest post has 100 likes. You might learn breaking news or you might find a hilarious video.

If you knew what was going to be in your feed, would you even bother checking it? Probably not! That's why Facebook refreshes and brings new items to your feed every second. They are trying to keep you engaged.

How to Implement: Discover ways you can continually surprise and delight your users! Do it repeatedly and add some variability to the mix. How can you create a craving and ongoing desire within your app?

Step #4: Investment

Investments are typically data, time, effort, social capital or money. When people are invested in your app, they become more likely to stay. Investments are made when a user puts something into the App. If users spend hours pinning posts to Pinterest, creating a music playlist on Spotify, or adding notes on Evernote, they become invested. The more time users spend on Facebook and Instagram, the more personalized the experience. The more invested the user is, the more inclined they are to continually use it. It's reported people spend more than 50 minutes a day across Facebook's suite of Apps including Instagram, Messenger, and Facebook.

Users are also less likely to use another App since their items are already saved on these apps. Take Snapchat as an example, users make an investment every time they take a selfie or record a video. When users are invested in the value creation aspect of an App, they enjoy it more. Therefore, they become more loyal. It's all about stored value.

How to Implement: Create ways to allow users to make investments that will improve the overall experience of the App. Add a feature that encourages and rewards more data, points, time, or money.

Instagram

Trigger

1. **External:** Push Notifications, Facebook & Twitter
   Internal: Fear of missing out

4. Build your own photo collectionto share, follow others, and comment

Reward

3. Connection and social proof

2. Take & post a photo

Investment

Action

Quizup

Trigger

1. **External:** Push notifications, Facebook + Twitter shares
   Internal: Entertainment & Socializing

4. Submit questions & grow your score

Reward

3. Compete with friends, win or lose

2. Take a quiz

Investment

Action

Spotify

Trigger

1. **External:** Facebook promotion
Internal: Feeling sad or happy

4. Build your own playlist and share them

Investment

Reward

3. New songs to listen to and discover

2. Press play

Action

Pinterest

Trigger

1. **External:** Emails and notifications
Internal: Feeling bored or fear of missing out

4. Build your own list of pins, follow others and comment

Investment

Reward

3. Discover new post and see what friends added

2. Login

Action

- Key Points -

➢ Measure marketing by only what is testable, measurable and scalable.

➢ Virality is not luck, it's engineered.

➢ Add viral features to your App from the beginning so every new user you acquire can bring in new additional engaged users at no cost to you.

➢ Make your App indispensable.

➢ Discover ways you can continually surprise and delight your users!

➢ A habit-forming product contains a Trigger, Routine Action, or some other form of Reward and Investment.

- Action Steps -

➢ What actions do your users take that increase their likelihood of returning to the app?

➢ How can you motivate the user to take an action that will also load the next future trigger?

➢ Brainstorm ways to surprise and delight your users.

➢ What internal Trigger does your user experience (boredom, loneliness, hunger, etc.) just before your intended habit?

➢ What are testable ways you can make an intended task easier for the user to complete?

➢ How can you create a craving and ongoing desire within your app?

➢ Discover what your users find most enjoyable about using your App and capitalize on it.

➢ Implement the "Viral App Blueprint" to dramatically increase downloads and sales.

What's Next?

How does Pokémon Go make $1 million a day? How does Candy Crush make $633,000 a day? In the following chapter, we'll dive deeper into the strategies of how to optimally monetize (make money) with your App. We'll uncover the secrets that the top Apps use to make incredible profits and how you can copy the same strategies for yourself.

CHAPTER 9

PILLAR 6: MONEY MASTERY

A s of 2017, Apple and Google have collectively paid out over $140 billion dollars to App creators. In this chapter, I'm going to walk you through exactly how you can get a piece of the billions that are paid out each year.

Business vs. Hobby

The unfortunate truth is that more than 85% of Apps on the market today are hobby apps. They do not have a sustainable business model. These App creators aren't in the business mindset. They are solely in the development mindset. That is also why (ironically) the same percentage of Apps fail within the first year. The reason they fail is they don't earn enough revenue to sustain the cost to market them. The App ends up with minimal downloads, draining both time and money.

If you don't have people who are using the App every single day and are willing to pay you for the value you provide, then what good is your development? Did you create the App just to create it, as a hobby? Or did you create it to provide value, get downloads and be financially compensated?

If you go into the App business with a business mindset versus a development mindset, you will set yourself up for success. If you can't figure out how to be self-sustaining from the revenue you make from the App; or from outside capital investment, you are destined to fail.

Many believe that they must create the most incredible product ever before they can make money from it. Those with a development mindset believe that the App must work 100% of the time, have no flaws and be jam packed with a ton of features before they figure out how to make money. Developers focus on building the most innovative product, but forget that the most creative and beautifully designed App doesn't necessarily translate into a moneymaker.

In fact, the average App launched doesn't have an effective way to make enough money to even cover the development costs. If you can implement a strong monetization strategy, you will automatically be far ahead of the competition.

Before you begin building the App it is important to first understand the science behind making the most income from your investment. What is the perceived value you are offering? How do you maximize that value to your user? How do you position your App so that users are not only interested in paying you, but will do so two, three, or even ten times over a year?

An App business requires a business model with the right pricing, right messaging and right delivery channel, to the right target customers. The key is to sell what your users want and then deliver what they need. This will not only keep your App alive, but will cause it to continue growing. Defining the right business model requires the same diligence as designing the right product, but the approach is much different. This will require putting your business financial hat on.

Look at the App ecosystem and imagine it as a game. Just like any game, there are rules and rewards. For you to reap the rewards, you must first understand how the game is played.

Having predictable revenue should be a primary goal.

APP SECRETS

The Truth About Building a Million Dollar App

The harsh reality is that although there has been more than $140 billion in App revenue paid out so far, just 1.6% of the 2.5 million Apps earn the majority of this revenue. Only 1.6% of all Apps are earning more than $500,000 per month. According to BusinessofApps.com, roughly 60% of Apps make less than $500 a each month. 23% make less than $100 per month. I want you to avoid being in these last two categories. I've routinely seen Apps fail because they lack an efficient strategy to monetize and acquire new users. I am going to show you how to sys-tematically make money from each new user and make more money from that user.

How Do Apps Make Money?

You can have the most ingenious mobile App of all time, but without a proper model to monetize and distribute it, your brilliant creation might remain your personal secret.

Choosing the right monetization strategy is important because it will determine the threshold of your app's financial potential. You can make $633,000 a day like Candy Crush, or less than $16 a day like the average App on the market. Different types of monetization methods can com-plement your app's functionality and purpose.

You may have to try more than one method. There are pros and cons to each method, so I recommend taking your time to test what strategy will be most profitable. To know which monetization method fits best you need to know how each works, and how each can be applied to dif-ferent types of apps.

The fundamental methods of how most Apps make money include: Paid, Freemium, Advertising and Subscription.

Paid Apps

Paid Apps are where a user must pay a one-time fee ranging from $1 to $100 to download the App. A few examples of the most successful paid Apps include Heads Up!, Afterlight, Plague Inc., and Minecraft (acquired by Microsoft for $2.5 Billion).

Although this may seem a logical option to make money, this is the most common mistake you can make. Repeat after me:

Big money is not made on the initial download.

Many developers create an App, imagining half a million people might download it at $1.99 each. Therefore, they expect it to make $1 million, minus the 30% fee incurred by Google and Apple. The problem with this philosophy is it usually doesn't work for two reasons:

Reason #1: Free Apps are in abundance. Paid Apps account for ONLY 10% of all downloads on the market. Users don't want to pay for Apps anymore. The percentage of paid Apps that users download has been decreasing every year.

Reason #2: It is not the most profitable approach. The most financially successful Apps on the market are free Apps that have In-App Purchase options. Why try to collect $1 dollar upfront when you can collect $10 (or potentially $100) dollars over time?

Freemium

Free Apps account for more than 90% of all App downloads. On average, nine of the top ten Apps on the market have a freemium strategy that utilizes In-App Purchases. This includes big shots like Uber, Snapchat, Airbnb, and Evernote. Even games like Candy Crush Saga and Angry Birds have a free model. Users now expect to try your App before spending money. It has become the standard for the industry.

With so many Apps fighting for the attention of a limited target market, the freemium model has become the new premium user experience. This model is an audition where the user is the talent scout: if you fail the audition and the user finds no value in your product, they have no problem seeking out better options. If your App nails the audition, you've got a role in their life and they will invest in your success. Give away some of your best stuff for free to "wow" your audience and build customer loyalty.

There are several ways Freemium Apps can earn revenue. This includes various forms of In-App Purchases. Examples are upgrades or speed-ups, buying services like a taxi or a massage, buying additional function-ality like levels or content, buying more time to use the App, paying to remove ads or a combination of all the above.

So again, nine times out of ten, a Freemium model is the way to go.

Advertising

In-App Advertising is a monetization model that is often combined with Freemium or Free-To-Play Apps. You make money every time a user en-gages (clicks or views) the advertisement inside your app. In general, users are willing to deal with ads in exchange for accessing your service or content at no cost. Billion dollar Apps like Snapchat, Facebook, and Instagram are great examples of offering a free App with In-App Adver-tising.

According to App Annie, an estimated 40% of Apps on the market are currently using In-App Advertising. Within your App, there are many types of ads that can be incorporated including: banner ads, interstitial ads, rich media ads and offer walls.

I. Banner Ads

Banner Ads are the easiest to produce. To include them, you can place a small banner sized ad on the top or bottom of the screen.

II. Interstitial Ads

These are ads laid over the entire screen. Typically, Interstitial Ads monetize better than Banner Ads do because they require users to interact with the ad by ultimately clicking the X button to close. Interstitial ads can easily replace a loading screen. The downside is these types of ads can be a significant "turnoff" to users and may affect your retention.

III. Rich Media Ads

Rich media ads display a video or play audio to the user. Studies have shown that quality rich media ads can keep a user's attention for 40-50 seconds. Since they're able to retain longer attention, they can be the most profitable. Just be cautious because bad media ads are the most annoying ads for users and can greatly effect your user retention.

IV. Offer Walls

Offer Walls give users rewards for interacting with ads. Frequently seen in gaming apps, these ads reward users with In-App currency and power-ups when they pass a level. These ads are effective because they give users an incentive to click on the ad.

Some users may dislike how invasive or distracting In-App Advertising can be. Specifically, with business-related apps, most users prefer an App with a user-friendly interface and a clean design to make them feel more organized. Therefore, it might be best to deviate from using In-App Advertising with business Apps to offer users the best experience.

In gaming apps, however, there is no such downside using Offer Walls since the user received a bonus of some sort.

Subscriptions

Subscriptions are where users pay a recurring amount of money (typically on a monthly or yearly basis) to access premium features or exclusive content during a specified timeframe. Examples include Billion Dollar Apps like Spotify, Pandora, and Netflix. Apps like WhatsApp, Tinder, and media outlets like the New York Times also use subscription models.

For example, the New York Times App allows you to view a limited number of articles but blocks the rest unless you pay to subscribe. The New York Times is a great example of how a product in a struggling industry is still managing to monetize and attract new users.

Subscriptions offer the benefit of a steady stream of income, but this model only works for Apps that continually offer fresh content. So, for this to work, you must offer new valuable content on a regular basis.

Monetization Is a Result of Engagement

The days of offering a paid App for $2, $5, or even $10 will soon be obsolete, apart from the gaming category. Users expect value before they are willing to pay for something. Therefore, making money and monetizing from an App must be a result of your users' positive engagement.

If the user is not engaged, they're not going to give you money to extend to the next level. The future of the App business is about building a long term relationship and providing continual value. When it comes time for that user to be further engaged, they are inspired to act and give you additional money for additional value.

The Law of Wealth

Business coach Dan Kennedy once said that the law of wealth is simply creating something that is more valuable to someone else than the money they are holding. When it comes to apps, it's all about the perceived value that you are offering. Provide something that is more valuable (perceived value) than the money your users have in their pocket (or digital wallet) and you will have a highly profitable App. It's that simple.

The Value Ladder

The key to maximizing revenue is to take the user through a process that provides continual value over time. This is what all-successful businesses (not just apps) call a Value Ladder. The concept is to take the user through a process that gives them more value through every stage of the relationship to a point where they begin to continually give you more and more money over time.

Value Ladder

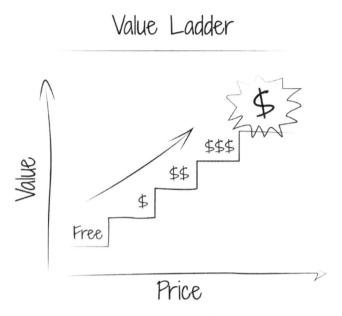

So, what's the point of a Value Ladder? The ultimate goal is to get the user to opt for your most expensive offer. This could be a "Buy All" or premium monthly subscription option. The problem with offering your most premium items upfront is that it's often too much of a commitment at the initial stage. Often one must earn the right to ask users to purchase the premium option.

Think of it this way. What if you went on a first date and proposed marriage to your partner. That would be crazy, right? What are the chances he or she would say yes to a lifetime commitment on the first date?

If the other person is interested in you after that first date, they will go on a second date and so on until they are eventually ready to marry you. Similarly, you can't expect your users to 'marry' your App after first downloading it. The concept is to ascend your users to the point where they are excited to purchase your premium offer. Take your users' vision and align it with your App. Have them fall in love with your solution more than their money.

What Is Lifetime Value?

Lifetime Value, also known as LTV, is your primary revenue metric. It represents the total financial value of your App to the consumer. It is how much money each App user generates in his or her lifetime.

It is the core revenue metric that all top Apps monitor. Uber is a great example. The App provides new users with a $25 credit upfront to use on rides. Why would Uber be willing to lose $25 upfront from every user? The answer is because they understand their Lifetime Value per user is far greater than $25. Shift your mindset from upfront income to long-term income.

I recommend viewing and splitting out your Lifetime Value information by average monthly value or value per customer and capturing their worth over time. It can also be tracked as revenue per customer, a slightly different formula that correlates directly to purchases, both In-App and across other channels to determine their overall spend. The key to having a high LTV is to keep users coming back for more by continually providing value, and maintaining high retention of your users.

Look at The Big Picture

By now I hope you are beginning to learn that the real money is not in the first transaction. When you understand how much a customer is worth over their lifetime, you know how much you can pay to acquire them. For Apps that have an equal number of downloads, there is a reason why certain Apps make a significant amount of money. Value is what creates income.

Value can be providing an additional level, features, product, services, or even merchandise. If you are operating on a certain level of value there is only a certain level of money you can make. I encourage you to constantly consider what additional value you can offer to your users.

The "10X Revenue Model"

Once your App has gained some traction and you have established a profitable business model, you can focus on maximizing your revenue opportunities. After analyzing the most highly profitable apps, I have uncovered several proven ways to exponentially increase revenues by using a system I call the "10X Revenue Model."

This 4-step model uses the same methods that billion dollar Apps like Tinder, Angry Birds, and Uber have incorporated to produce millions in additional revenue. Our clients have incorporated these techniques resulting in 10X revenues and they will work for you as well.

10X Revenue Model

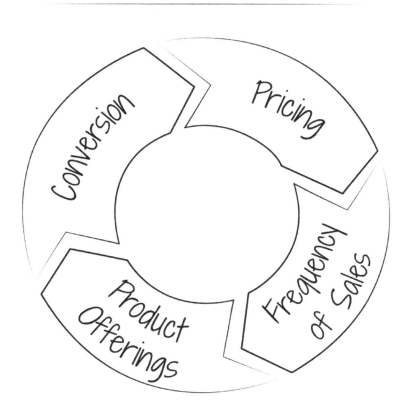

Step #1: Increase Sales Conversions

Increasing your sales conversions involves focusing on increasing the number of free users into paid users. This process requires tweaking how you market and present your offerings. Based on the category your App is in and optimizing the sales copy of your In-App Purchase offers, you can expect anywhere between 2%-10% of your users to convert into purchasers.

It is critical to strategically guide users to your offer. Your offer must be easily available and irresistible. Many developers make the mistake of having their In-App Purchases buried within the App making them hard to find or even difficult to understand. Consider how you can improve the language of your offers to best convey the benefits you are offering versus the features.

When introducing users to your offers, it is important to entice them towards your higher priced option. Often the best way is with a perceived discount. When it comes to In-App Purchase options, many simply lay out different offers with each one going up proportionately with the same price increase for each option.

For example:

- Unlock Level 1: $0.99

- Unlock Level 2: $1.99

- Unlock Level 3: $2.99

This is a mistake. I have found that by modifying pricing options to have one option with a higher perceived value at a discounted cost can drastically boost profits.

For example, Angry Birds has the following options:

- 80 Points: $0.99

- 400 Points: $4.99

- 2100 Points: $9.99

The third option is profoundly discounted and has a far greater perceived value. It is essential to understand the science behind how the most profitable Apps make money. The Angry Birds Franchise, owned by Rovio, makes roughly 30% of their sales from In-App purchases, and is currently valued at $2 billion dollars.

The users should not have to calculate your great deal. Tell them! Explicitly highlight that your offer is XX% off. Too many Apps offer a discount but don't explicitly highlight it. The result is they miss out on increased conversions and profits because the user isn't fully aware of how great the offer is. Multi-millionaire entrepreneur and legendary copywriter Dan Kennedy once said, "You're just one sales copy away from being rich." A few simple tweaks to your marketing language and your In-App purchase offerings can be the difference between making hundreds or thousands more per day.

The key to finding the best marketing language and pricing layout is to do A/B testing. You must test and see what works best by constantly improving your offers. Remember, you can't improve what you don't track.

Step #2: Increase Your Prices & Premium Offerings

If you increase your prices, you will increase sales. This may sound like common sense but it's not common practice. Users that are more inclined to make In-App Purchases are also willing to pay more for them. I encourage you to maximize your prices and provide premium offerings.

Angry Birds offers 13,000 Points for $99; Tinder offers 60 Super Likes for $40; and Uber offers the Black Car starting at $15. Does your App offer a premium option? What is the most expensive item you can offer to your users?

Many Apps undervalue themselves by not having premium offers and therefore never reach their full revenue potential. Boosting your prices and providing premium offers can be easily incorporated and drive extraordinary results.

Step #3: Increase Frequency of Sales Per User

This method focuses on increasing the number of purchases from each user. According to the Gartner Group, 80 percent of your future profits will come from just 20 percent of your existing customers. That means the revenue sources you've been trying to find are likely sitting right under your nose! Nurture and cultivate your existing sources to their maximum potential.

Additionally, the market research agency, Marketing Metrics, stated that 70% of users who make one In-App Purchase are more inclined to purchase again. This can be encouraged through ongoing direct marketing efforts such as using push notifications, promotional videos, facebook retargeting, and even email. Remember that the key is to entice the user towards purchasing the high-priced options at a perceived discount!

I recommend having a "Buy All" option at a discounted price. You rarely see people make purchase decisions in absolute terms. We mostly rely on comparisons between options to make a purchase decision and "Buy All" is some users go-to strategy in Apps.

Give users an offer they simply can't refuse. People often anchor to one piece of information when making a future decision. Therefore, if you show that the user is getting a great deal, they will select it. We have seen Apps more than triple their revenue by adding an "Unlock All" or "Buy All" option at a discounted price.

Although the total number of purchases may be less, the "Unlock All" or "Buy All" options have proven to be the highest revenue option for many apps. With this option, you benefit by receiving full payment today, rather than waiting for payments tomorrow. The user benefits by gaining access to all your content at once, at a discounted price!

Step #4: Increase Your Product Offerings

What else can your App offer? By strategically combining multiple business models into your App, you start to open new revenue opportunities. Uber offers one-time transportation options (Uber Pool, UberX, Black Car) at different incentivized pricing. However, they now also offer a subscription model providing unlimited Uber Pool rides at a flat monthly fee.

Tinder not only uses both In-App Advertising and In-App Purchase options, but also offers a subscription service called Tinder Plus. Tinder Plus provides additional value such as Unlimited Swipes and extra Super Likes for a flat monthly rate. According to Credit Suisse, Tinder has over 100,000 Tinder Plus subscribers and is currently valued at over $3 billion.

Many of the top Apps incorporate a variety of product offerings and you should too. It is reported that over 50% of Angry Birds revenue is now outside of the App from licensing deals and merchandising. If you focus on building a community that your users want to be a part of, they are far more inclined to purchase your different offerings. I encourage you to foster a loyal community that would be inclined to wear a shirt with your icon or character on it just as others do with Angry Birds and Clash of Clans. By incorporating the right product offering to your App you can easily double or triple existing profits. Build a brand, not just an App!

Want Others to Invest in Your App Business?

Most startups have trouble raising investment. What is the best way to get investors interested in your app? The answer is to make money. Only 1% of all new startups ever get funded. Stop waiting for investors to save you. If your product is good enough, you should be able to generate sales from it.

You can then go to the investor community and tell investors your app is worth their investing in since you have proven your App has reached a Product-Market-Fit and you have the downloads and sales to back up that claim. Unless you can generate sales, you have an expensive hobby. Sales are the key to the highest level of success.

- Key Points -

➢ The future of the App business is about building a relationship and providing continual value so that when it comes time for that user to be further engaged, they are inspired to act and give you money for additional value.

➢ If you can't figure out how to be self-sustaining from the revenue you make from the App or outside capital investment, you are destined to fail.

➢ An App business requires an equally elegant business model with the right pricing, messaging and delivery channel to the right target customers.

➢ Sell what your users want and deliver what they most need.

➢ Big money is not made on the initial download.

➢ Incorporate the right offers into your App and you can easily double, or even triple existing profits.

➢ The key to maximizing revenue is to take the user through a process (Value Ladder) that provides continual value over time.

➢ Build a brand, not just an App!

- Action Steps -

➢ What is the perceived value you are trying to offer?

➢ What is the most profitable way to monetize your app?

➢ How can you maximize value to your user?

➢ How can you position your App so users are not only interested in paying you, but will do so two, three, or even ten times over a year?

➢ What is the Lifetime Value per user?

➢ What additional products or benefits can you offer that can be used to monetize your app?

➢ Incorporate the "10X Revenue Model" and see your sales sky-rocket.

What's Next?

How do you measure success? You can't build a million dollar App without understanding key metrics that are used to track and grow it. In the following chapters, I'll uncover the 5-key metrics that you can easily track. I'm going to show you the system you can use to track and understand your App analytics in just 20-minutes a day so that you can work smarter, not harder.

CHAPTER 10

PILLAR 7: MEASURING SUCCESS

How do you measure the success of an app? What do you define as success? Without tracking your growth or decline, you won't fully understand how to improve it. When you think about marketing, what's the first thing that comes to mind? Is it catchy taglines like Nike's "Just Do It", Super Bowl commercials, Times Square Billboards or Facebook Ads? What the most successful marketers understand is that every effective marketing initiative starts with understanding the core success <u>metrics</u> behind every marketing campaign.

You Can't Improve What You Don't Track

As an App creator, you most likely spend significant time each week on development and marketing your App. What if you found out your development advancements and marketing efforts were not bringing you any more downloads? You would probably change your efforts. Right?

The truth is your App marketing initiatives probably follow the 80/20 rule. In other words, 20% of the marketing you do accounts for 80% of the additional downloads you get. If that's the case, it becomes important to identify which 20% it is so you can do more of what works and less of what doesn't work.

Optimize or Become Irrelevant

When tracking Uber's revenue and retention, Uber found that the more that a rider utilizes Uber, the less willing they are to wait for a car to arrive and pick them up. Analytics showed that in 2013, users were willing to wait 12 minutes for an Uber car to arrive before canceling. Yet just one year later, they were only willing to wait 8 minutes before cancelling. For Uber, if they had never tracked this performance metric, it would have resulted in a loss of millions of dollars per month.

Uber needed to continually raise the bar to improve their users' experience to stay competitive and retain users. If they did not continually track and improve the time it took for a car to arrive, many people would simply switch to a competing ride sharing App.

Given this data, it's safe to say the next billion-dollar App to compete with Uber will be competing on the user experience and transportation efficiency. That is the time it takes for a car to arrive and transport the user to their destination.

Don't Be Lazy, Test Like Crazy

You might be thinking, 'I don't have a billion dollar App yet so I don't need to track it.'

On the contrary, many developers launch their App, yet only monitor their number of downloads and sales. This is where many Apps fail. Without tracking key performance metrics, you won't understand what's driving downloads, where your engaged users come from, nor what's driving revenues.

Studies have shown that Apps using App analytics outperform competitors who just trust their intuition at a 3 to 1 ratio. Your analytics is your roadmap to success. The data behind your analytics will leave you breadcrumbs to follow. If you follow them, they will lead you to the Promised Land. Analytics allow you to understand what works and doesn't to obtain actionable insight you can begin incorporating into your App right away.

In 2002, there was an American baseball team called the Oakland A's. They were a mediocre team without a lot money. Billy Beane, the general manager of the A's, one day had an epiphany. Baseball's conventional wisdom was all-wrong.

Faced with a tight budget, Beane reinvented his team by outsmarting the more well-funded teams. Joining forces with Ivy League graduate Peter Brand, Beane challenged old-school traditions by recruiting bargain players whom the scouts labeled as flawed but had statistically shown game-winning potential. Using analytics, Beane beat the system. He took a team of "average" players and won 20 consecutive games, setting an American League record. His team beat several richer teams and entered the play-offs that year. His system was so popular it had its own label called Sabermetrics.

If you master the analytics and data behind your App, you can beat the system and outperform your competitors. To become a master in App marketing, you must master analytics because they go hand-in-hand. You can get 1 million downloads, but without understanding where, why and how users find and interact with the App, you are in jeopardy of having a one-hit wonder.

When it comes to business metrics, you need to make data meaningful. The key is to understand which core metrics are most important to you. There is an overwhelming amount of data to understand and track, but the data points, without context, are useless. You must understand what they mean for it to be valuable. Once you understand what it means, you can act to improve your App and increase downloads.

Make the Data Meaningful

I meet with many developers that can tell me certain metrics about their App. For example, they know they had 20,000 downloads last month and $4,000 in sales. That's good information, but they don't know anything else about the App. The key is to dive deeper and look for insights you can use to get more downloads and sales.

If that same person told me 10,000 of their 20,000 downloads came from Facebook advertising and that accounted for 50% of their total sales, we would have more actionable insight into how to market the App going forward. We could drill deeper into the app's retention, engagement and drop off rates to see opportunities to further skyrocket downloads and sales.

Measure Your Efforts

It's A Simple Question...
Did Our Marketing
Campaign Drive
Downloads Or Not?

Oh
sh*t...

Metrics That Matter

There are key indicators of performance that most often affect the bottom line. The lens you should look at your App business through can be broken down into 2 core focus points; Downloads and Conversions.

Downloads - includes your marketing initiatives that drive users to download the App. These include Acquisition and Activation (we'll cover this in more detail).

Conversions - This includes Revenue (LTV), Retention and Referrals

These are the action items that most matter. If you were to break down your daily action items and those actions are not correlated to getting more downloads and increased conversion, then you need to really ask, why are you taking that action?

It is important to examine it like a funnel. Your job is to understand which stage your users are currently in. Success is measured by the difference in each stage. There is a conversion rate you can track for each stage. You want to entice the customer to the next stage of the funnel... to ultimately pay you and continue to come back for more.

Analytics Framework

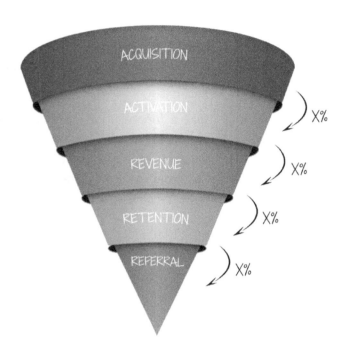

Five Key Metrics to Track & Grow Your App

In the following section, I outline the core framework of the 5 most important App analytics to track and improve your App. After analyzing and working with more than 3,000 apps, I found what the most successful Apps track. They ALL track (and improve) at least five of the same core metrics. This is the system all the top Apps monitor to increase downloads, enhance user engagement and boost revenue.

I want you to work smarter, not harder. Here is a system you can use to track and understand your App analytics in just 20 minutes each day. I recommend having intuitive dashboards set up to monitor and track these for you.

#1 ACQUISITION

"Where Do Your Downloads Come From?"

Acquisition refers to the process of attracting users to download your App. It allows you to understand the vitally important information of where your downloads came from. If you know what type of users you have attracted and where they are coming from, you will be able to better define your niche, improve your marketing tactics and drive more of these types of users to your App. A better-defined niche leads to specific targeted marketing, resulting in a higher download conversion. If you are more accurate in knowing what about your App attracts customers, you will get more downloads while spending less time, energy and money to aquire them.

#2 ACTIVATION

"Are They Actually Using the App?"

Activation refers to the percentage of people who use the App after downloading it. According to the analytics agency Localytics, roughly 22% of Apps are downloaded and used just once. The key is to deliver an experience people will never forget. Ask yourself, 'How can I "wow" the user within the first 30 seconds of opening my App for the first time?

Having an extraordinary first impression is essential. Successfully driving downloads is the goal, but what good is getting downloads if they don't use the app more than once? The activation percentage can quickly tell you whether the App leaves your user feeling enticed and motivated or... uninterested.

#3 RETENTION

"Are People Coming Back?"

Retention is measured by how many users revisit your App over a certain period. Retention is the single most important metric for measuring growth and longevity. By analyzing retention, you can determine the percentage of people who have a good initial experience. Furthermore, you can determine how many of those users never return.

Localytics reported there is only a 60% chance a user will return to your App if it has not been used within a week. Analyzing retention demonstrates the importance of keeping customers continually interested and engaged in your product or service.

A high retention rate means you are satisfying the customers' needs. So how do you improve your retention and keep users coming back for more? Are the users who download your App staying for the long term?

High retention comes when there is a great Product-Market-Fit. At a Stanford University lecture, the head of growth at Facebook, Alex Schultz shared, "Think about what the magic moment (wow effect) is for your product and get people connected to it as fast as possible. You can go from 20% retention to 60% retention easily if you connect people with 'The thing' that makes them stick to using your product."

Consider how you can build loyalty with your users and make your App indispensable to them. Simon Sinek, author of 'Start With Why,' once said, "Loyalty is not a program; loyalty is a feeling. Loyalty means that we are willing to suffer inconvenience to continue to choose to do business with you. We will pay more, travel further and give you the benefit of the doubt. Loyalty is not rational. Loyalty is emotional. It's more than a motivation; it's inspiration. We are loyal to the brands, organizations, and people with whom we connect on an emotional level."

#4 REFERRAL

"Are People Sharing the App?"

Referrals show the percentage of users who share and refer a friend to your App. Having a good referral campaign can cause a chain reaction of promotion among users and make your App go viral very quickly. Enticing users to promote your App can be done by offering a win-win referral strategy. As mentioned in the previous chapter on Virality, for example, the mobile App Lyft gives a $20 ride credit when a user refers a friend to sign up for the service. These tactics are proven to work.

#5 LIFETIME VALUE

"How Much Money Are You Making Per User?"

How can Apps like Lyft, Uber, Grubhub, and many others afford to give out $10- $25 credit to first time users? The answer is the Lifetime Value per user is far greater, two-five times, than the initial customer acquisition cost. Remember, Lifetime Value refers to the total amount of revenue that a customer will contribute to your App over the entire customer life cycle.

It compares the value of a single user to all other customers. Tracking and analyzing the Lifetime Value of a consumer is the most important metric because it allows you to pinpoint your best customers, optimize your budget and understand the overall revenue health of your App.

According to Flurry's data, the average U.S. user spends 2 hours and 42 minutes per day on mobile devices. 86% of that time is spent in apps. But, not all customers are profitable. Here comes that famous 80/20 principle again: 20% of your customers provide 80% of your profit. Identifying your best customers allows you to create customer loyalty programs. The key is for you to segment the most profitable customer groups and develop your customer loyalty programs to retain them. Your LTV offers a more effective way to optimize your spending over the long term.

Optimizing your budget to save money and spend where it matters is something all successful business seek. LTV is a useful tool that helps differentiate repeat purchasers from their less lucrative peers. When you understand these metrics, you can optimize acquisition spending for maximum value.

What if you can get a user to spend 10 times more than others, but it costs slightly more to market to them? Will you spend more on marketing to them to download your app? The answer is obviously YES. You can also compare LTV across channels, and ads within channels, to maximize every penny you spend. If you'd like to go deeper into measuring and improving your App, I've put together a video for you called the App Analytics Blueprint. Simply go to AppMarketingAcademy.com/Analytics to check it out.

- Key Points -

➤ The five-core metrics to track and improve your App are: Acquisition, Activation, Retention, Referral and Lifetime Value.

➤ Customer Lifetime Value (LTV) is considered one of the most meaningful metrics for evaluating the profitability of an App

➤ Don't be lazy, test like crazy.

➤ Continue to measure and optimize or become irrelevant.

➤ When it comes to analytics and understanding your key performance indicators, having context is key.

- Action Steps -

➤ What metrics matter most to you?

➤ How can you "wow" the user within the first 30 seconds of opening the App for the first time?'

➤ When examining your analytics, where is your App lacking?

➤ What sort of referral campaign could you implement in your app?

➤ How can you improve your retention and keep users coming back for more?

➤ How can you shorten the signup process? What's really required for the user to get value required? Is it possible to sign up with just one click?

THE FUTURE OF APPS

The only thing certain in the future for mobile devices is change. However, what is clear is that Apps will continue to be the medium of the future. Apps are here to stay. Devices may change, but Apps will be the software that runs on any hardware that arises. What is also clear is new Apps are hitting the billion-dollar valuation mark every 6 months. This will grow at an increasing rate in the future.

The time it takes to create a billion-dollar App will shrink as new social channels arise to share apps. New Apps will go viral with 100+ million users in a matter of days or minutes. Pokémon Go grew from 0 - 200 million downloads in just 4 months. Now with 100's of millions of new smartphone devices introduced around the world monthly, the opportunity and growth for apps is just beginning.

Regarding the interfaces and devices Apps will run on, there is no doubt that cyberspace will spill over into the physical world. We see this via the 'Internet of Things,' a world where smart TV's, self-driving cars, smart watches and smart homes grow and expand. With the help of Augmented/Virtual Reality and embedded sensors around us, computers and phones will morph into our everyday objects.

In the years to come, computation will not just be a single hardware. The new age has an intrinsic quality within everything that surrounds us. Ever-evolving sensors will be embedded round us, making us interconnected with the Apps we use.

We are in the "Information Age." My guess is that the new era will be called the "Connective Age." Wired Magazine co-founder Kevin Kelly said, "Now that we have the burst of mass information introduced through the advent of the internet and technology, the next leap forward is that we are essentially cognizing the world."

We are empowering our surroundings with technologies that will give it even more life. We are only beginning to see it with smart electronics. Just as we energized the world with electricity and the light bulb, we are impregnating the world with a mind of its own through software and connective technology.

We use wearable's that have situational awareness. In this Connective Age that is unfolding, more of the world around us will come alive. Our preferences will become embedded dynamically with our surroundings and how we respond to the world around us. They will anticipate our needs by understanding our own context.

The future of Apps is incredibly exciting. As Peter Drucker once said, "The best way to predict the future is to create it."

Now is your time to turn your App dream into a reality. Create it!

Apps Let You Reach for The Stars

Two graduates from Stanford with minds sharp and eyes wide open stepped into the world of Silicon Valley. They were well-prepared, but inexperienced. They worked at different companies for years honing their skills. One day they felt they were ready to go out and build something on their own.

They saw that the App Industry was full of possibilities and ended up creating the first billion-dollar App. Kevin Systrom and Mike Krieger turned mediocre photographers (almost every one of us) into Gods of the camera and interact with others in a creative new way. They used filters and allowed everyone to present themselves exactly the way they wanted. Systrom and Krieger transformed Instagram from an overly ambitious, location based social network into what it is today with a simple, yet brilliant twist.

If you look at all the Apps that are currently on the market anything you can think of most likely exists in one form or another. But that doesn't mean everything has already been invented. That doesn't mean there are no gaps in the market.

On the contrary, many of the new, most successful Apps do the same thing as existing Apps, but with a twist. And it's that twist that ignites growth and allows an App to reach extraordinary success. The industry allows absolutely anyone with a great idea, financial backing and a great team to succeed.

In the beginning, I believed having Dyslexia was a flaw. It wasn't until years later that I began to realize that like any flaw or problem, there is a solution or benefit on the other side. I began to realize that my defined flaw would turn out to be my super power. Research has discovered that individuals with Dyslexia tend to be more creative and innovative. I discovered although Dyslexia sometimes affects my ability to read and with mathematics, there also comes my greater ability to think in creative ways.

This has allowed me to create innovative products and market them in a unique and successful way. I later discovered that in fact some of the most successful and wealthiest visionaries had Dyslexia like my idols Steve Jobs, Henry Ford, and Richard Branson.

Whatever it is that is currently stopping you from experiencing the lifestyle of your dreams, whether it is a lack of time, finances, education, age or environment, I am here to tell you that you can do this. Discover how you can turn your current circumstance into your super power. If it is a lack of time, I have seen successful Apps built and launched in less than 7 days. If it is finances, I have seen Apps built for less than $100 dollars. If it is your age, the youngest App creator has been 8 years old and the oldest has been 80. If they can do it, so can you! Don't let anything stand in the way of fulfilling your dreams.

If you faithfully incorporate the "App Secrets" laid out for you throughout this book, you will be on a path to building the next Million Dollar and even Billion Dollar App business. For some it will come soon. For MOST it will take time, commitment and action. Remember, the right actions, persisted over time, guarantees your success.

By now you know it doesn't matter how much you learn... if you don't use what you learn. Many believe knowledge is power. This is false. Knowledge is not power, but potential power. If you don't put what you have learned to work, it is useless. I encourage you to take your super powers which are your unique abilities and unleash them into the world. Be steadfast. Your success will always be measured by the quality and quantity of the service you render to others.

I am truly humbled by the opportunity to share my "App Secrets" with you as you set out to dominate the App world. The mobile App world has been my vehicle to live the lifestyle of my dreams. Now it is time for you to act and pursue your dreams. With the right coaching and taking the right actions over time, your success is inevitable. I wish you all the best.

APPENDIX

Become the Next Successful App Creator

If you want to be a part of a group of individuals taking step-by-step actions on a daily basis to turn their app dream into reality, then make sure that you get on the waitlist for the next round of enrollment into the App Marketing Academy. This is where I go in and coach a group of passionate individuals looking to take their life and their App to a whole new level. Visit the website www.AppMarketingAcademy.com now to learn more and join our next class.

Want To Work With An Expert?

How would you like to DOUBLE, TRIPLE, or even 10X your App downloads? Do you have an App or are in the process of launching your App and have a marketing budget $10,000 or more? PreApps has helped thousands of Apps over the years reach millions of downloads. We can help you too. For more details simply visit www.PreApps.com/App-Marketing-Services and schedule a FREE 30-Minute Breakthrough App Strategy Call.

Have Sean Speak At Your Next Event!

Want Sean Casto to speak at your next event or board meeting? Casto is one of the most in-demand speakers on mobile App marketing growth. He has been a guest speaker at industry conventions for Microsoft and Samsung and lectured at Northeastern and Harvard Universities. His combination of inspiration, comedic style humor and proven results-oriented strategies add up to an experience your attendees will thank you for repeatedly...and never forget! For inquiries and availability, visit SeanCasto.com

- RESOURCES -

Need Help Marketing Your App?
Want to Double, Triple, or even 10X your app growth? PreApps can help you.
www.preapps.com/app-marketing-services/

Join Our Free Workshop!
Want to learn how to create a Million Dollar app? Register for the next online workshop!
www.AppMarketingAcadmey.com

Create Million Dollar App Screenshots
Want to create high converting beautifully designed app screenshots for your app? Get instant access to the best App Screenshot design tool on the market.
www.AppScreenshots.co

- REFERENCES -

Ryan Holiday, Growth Hacker Marketing. Profile Books Ltd, 2014.

Andrew Chen, "Growth Hacker Is the New VP Marketing." Andrewchen.co, 21 Oct. 2016, andrewchen.co/how-to-be-a-growth-hacker-an-airbnbcraigslist-case-study/.

Harnish, Verne. Scaling up: How a Few Companies Make It ... and Why the Rest Don't. Gazelles Inc., 2015.

Adam L. Penenberg, Viral Loop: from Facebook to Twitter, How Today's Smartest Businesses Grow Themselves. Hyperion, 2009.

Christine Lagorio-Chafkin, "Brian Chesky, Joe Gebbia, and Nathan Blecharczyk, Founders of AirBnB." Inc.com, Inc., 19 July 2010, www.inc.com/30under30/2010/profile-brian-chesky-joe-gebbia-nathan-blecharczyk-airbnb.html

Marc Andreesen, "EE204: Business Management for Electrical Engineers and Computer Scientists." EE204 Business Management for Engineers and Computer Scientists, Standford, 25 June 2007, web.stanford.edu/class/ee204/ProductMarketFit.html.

Jonah Berger, Contagious: Why Things Catch On. Simon & Schuster Paperbacks, 2016.

Anthony Ha, "Dropbox CEO: Why Search Advertising Failed Us." VentureBeat, 27 Oct. 2010, venturebeat.com/2010/10/27/dropbox-drew-houston-adwords/.

George Lois, Damn Good Advice For People With Talent. Phaidon Inc Ltd, 2012.

Mureta, Chad. App Empire. Wiley India Pvt Ltd.

George Berkowski, How to Build a Billion Dollar App: Discover the Secrets of the Most Successful Entrepreneurs of Our Time. Piatkus Books, 2014.

Walter Isaacson, Steve Jobs. Universal Studios, 2015.

Nir Eyal, and Ryan Hoover. Hooked: How to Build Habit-Forming Products. Princeton University Press, 2014.

Gabriel Weinberg, Traction. Portfolio Penguin, 2016.

Perez, Sarah. "Consumers Spend 85% Of Time On Smartphones In Apps, But Only 5 Apps See Heavy Use." TechCrunch, TechCrunch, 22 June 2015

Nachum, Gal. "Milestone-Based Vesting For Startup Founders." TechCrunch, TechCrunch, 9 Dec. 2015, techcrunch.com/2015/12/09/milestone-based-vesting-for-startup-founders/.

Brunson, Russell, and Robert T. Kiyosaki. Expert Secrets: the Underground Playbook to Find Your Message, Build a Tribe, and Change the World... MJ, 2017.

Sean Ellis, and Morgan Brown. Hacking Growth: How Today's Fastest-Growing Companies Drive Breakout Success. Crown Business, 2017.

"Market Metrics." Market Metrics, Market Metrics, 18 Mar. 2015, www.marketmetrics.com/.

Arash, Drew. "Celebrating Half a Billion Users." Dropbox Blog, Dropbox, 7 Mar. 2017, blogs.dropbox.com/dropbox/2016/03/500-million/.

"Dropbox's Referral Program – How They Got 4 Million Users In 15 Months." Word-of-Mouth and Referral Marketing Blog, Referral Candy, 29 May 2017, www.referralcandy.com/blog/dropbox-referral-program/.

Patel, Neil. "Kissmetrics Blog." 5 Myths About App Store Optimization (ASO), Neil Patel, 22 June 2014, blog.kissmetrics.com/5-myths-about-aso/.

"Mobile Marketing Statistics Compilation." Smart In-sights, Smartinsights, 17 May 2017, www.smartinsights.com/mobile-marketing/mobile-marketing-analytics/mobile-marketing-statistics/.

Haden, Jeff. "With 5 Words, Bruce Springsteen Taught Beats Co-Founder Jimmy Iovine a Life-Changing Lesson in Teamwork." Inc.com, Inc., www.inc.com/jeff-haden/with-5-words-bruce-springsteen-taught-the-co-found.html.

Bellis, Rich. "The Right Way To Pick A Cofounder For Your Startup." Fast Company, Fast Company, 16 Dec. 2015, www.fastcompany.com/3054583/four-essential-criteria-for-picking-a-cofounder.

Gilbert, David. "Rovio's 'Overnight' Success with Angry Birds Came After 51 Failed Attempts." International Business Times UK, Ibtimes, 1 July 2014, www.ibtimes.co.uk/rovio-overnight-angry-brids-success-51-failed-522587.

Robbins, Tony. "The Tony Robbins Podcast by Tony Robbins on Apple Podcasts." Apple Podcasts, ITunes, itunes.apple.com/us/podcast/the-tony-robbins-podcast/id1098413063?mt=2.

Polish, Joe. "I Love Marketing with Joe Polish and Dean Jackson by Joe Polish and Dean Jackson on Apple Podcasts." Apple Podcasts, ITunes, itunes.apple.com/us/podcast/i-love-marketing-with-joe-polish-and-dean-jackson/id412684163?mt=2.

Fishburne, Tom. "Marketoonist | Tom Fishburne." Marketoonist | Tom Fishburne, Marketoonis, marketoonist.com/.

Perez, Sarah. "Consumers Spend 85% Of Time On Smartphones In Apps, But Only 5 Apps See Heavy Use." TechCrunch, TechCrunch, 22 June 2015, techcrunch.com/2015/06/22/consumers-spend-85-of-time-on-smartphones-in-apps-but-only-5-apps-see-heavy-use/.

Huet, Ellen. "Uber Says It's Doing 1 Million Rides Per Day, 140 Million In Last Year." Forbes, Forbes Magazine, 17 Dec. 2014, www.forbes.com/sites/ellenhuet/2014/12/17/uber-says-its-doing-1-million-rides-per-day-140-million-in-last-year/#5260b05152cd.

Flynn, Kerry. "How Many People Are On Tinder? Company Defends With 'Actual Data' In Vanity Fair Comeback." International Business Times, Ibtimes, 12 Aug. 2015, www.ibtimes.com/how-many-people-are-tinder-company-defends-actual-data-vanity-fair-comeback-2050092.

Kalanic, Travis. "Uber's Biggest Launch to Date?" Uber.com, Uber, 22 Sept. 2011, www.uber.com/blog/chicago/chicago-ubers-biggest-launch-to-date/.

Koch, Richard, and Greg Lockwood. Simplify. Piatkus Books, 2016.

Stern, Joanna. "Cellphone Users Check Phones 150x/Day and Other Internet Fun Facts."ABC News, ABC News Network, 29 May 2013, abcnews.go.com/blogs/technology/2013/05/cellphone-users-check-phones-150xday-and-other-internet-fun-facts/.

Ries, Eric. Lean Startup. Portfolio Penguin, 2017.

Maxwell, John. "John Maxwell on Leadership." JohnMaxwell.com, The John Maxwell Company, 1 Oct. 2014, www.johnmaxwell.com/blog/man-in-the-mirror.

- Notes -

- Notes -

- Notes -

Made in United States
Orlando, FL
23 December 2023

41010817R00104